Engraving of Powell Expedition in Grand Canyon by artist R. A. Muller

RIVER MASTER

RIVER MASTER

★ ★ ★ ★

John Wesley Powell's
Legendary Exploration of the
Colorado River and Grand Canyon

Cecil Kuhne

THE COUNTRYMAN PRESS
A division of W. W. Norton & Company
Independent Publishers Since 1923

All photos courtesy of the National Parks Service. Engravings and illustrations originally appeared in *The Exploration of the Colorado River and Its Canyons* by John Wesley Powell, first published in 1875.

For information about permission to reproduce selections from this book, write to Permissions, The Countryman Press, 500 Fifth Avenue, New York, NY 10110

For information about special discounts for bulk purchases, please contact W. W. Norton Special Sales at specialsales@wwnorton.com or 800-233-4830

Manufacturing by LSC Communications, Harrisonburg
Book design by Lovedog Studio
Production manager: Devon Zahn

The Countryman Press
www.countrymanpress.com

A division of W. W. Norton & Company, Inc.
500 Fifth Avenue, New York, NY 10110
www.wwnorton.com

Library of Congress Cataloging-in-Publication Data

Names: Kuhne, Cecil C., III, 1952- author.
Title: River master : John Wesley Powell's legendary exploration of the Colorado River and Grand Canyon / Cecil Kuhne.
Description: New York, NY : The Countryman Press, 2017. | Includes bibliographical references and index.
Identifiers: LCCN 2017025435 | ISBN 9781682680742 (hardcover)
Subjects: LCSH: Powell, John Wesley, 1834–1902—Travel—Colorado River (Colo.-Mexico) | Powell, John Wesley, 1834–1902—Travel—Arizona—Grand Canyon. | Colorado River (Colo.-Mexico)—Discovery and exploration. | Grand Canyon (Ariz.)—Discovery and exploration | Explorers—Colorado River (Colo.-Mexico)—Biography. | Explorers—Arizona—Grand Canyon—Biography.
Classification: LCC F788 .K94 2017 | DDC 910.92 [B] —dc23
LC record available at http://lccn.loc.gov/2017025435

10 9 8 7 6 5 4 3 2 1

To Clare

CONTENTS

"Time is a sort of river of passing events, and strong is its current; no sooner is a thing brought to sight than it is swept by and another takes its place, and this too will be swept away."

—Marcus Aurelius

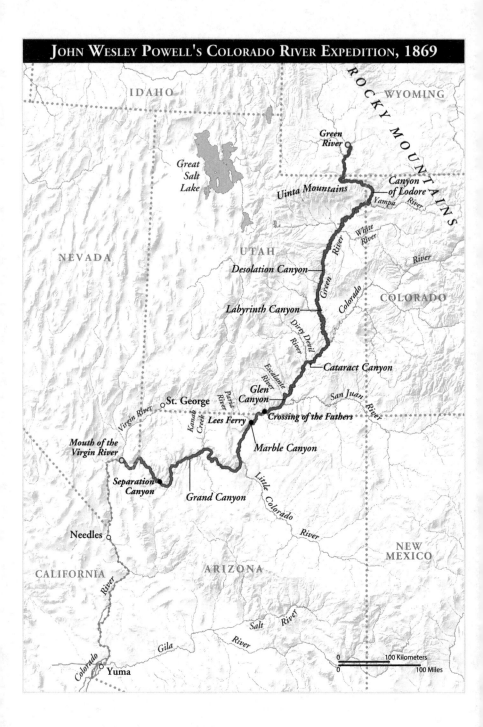

JOHN WESLEY POWELL'S COLORADO RIVER EXPEDITION, 1869

PROLOGUE

THE CHALLENGING RAPIDS THAT ROAR NOISILY within its deep, secluded canyons have made the mighty whitewater rivers of the American West justifiably famous among river runners. None of these glistening liquid gems are more renowned than the Green and Colorado Rivers, born among the airy, snow-covered peaks of Wyoming, Utah, and Colorado. The trickling headwaters of these two streams spring forth from the craggy 13,000- and 14,000-foot heights of the Wind River, Uinta, Wasatch, and Rocky Mountain Ranges, and their rivulets wend their way downstream until they finally merge, pulsing through the vast Colorado Plateau and a series of stark and hauntingly beautiful corridors.

The enticing landscape that is found here has been described by historian and noted Colorado River explorer Robert Brewster Stanton as "full of strange forms and changing colors which inspire awe, wonder, and amazement, a country in which at every turn one is startled by scenes of grandeur beyond compare, of beauty beyond conception, of coloring so bold, so wild, and yet so delicate and harmonious as to turn an artist's brain with despair of being able to catch the mystic, hazy tints of opal, topaz, mauve, pink, and lilac that hang over its deserts, its mountains, and its canyoned gorges." To stand on the shores of wild and majestic natural forces such as these, peer into the closing walls of the lonely and unexplored chasms downstream, and then abruptly shove a boat into the quickening current is clearly not an undertaking for the faint of heart.

An intrepid, but remarkably scruffy, band of ten men—known officially to the world as the Colorado River Exploring Expedition—did just that as they launched four long, heavily laden wooden rowboats from the dusty banks of the Green River in southern Wyoming. It was the early afternoon of May 24, 1869, and their leader was John Wesley Powell, an ambitiously driven geology professor and former Union major who had lost most of his right arm in the Battle of Shiloh.

With the group's four boats—christened the *Emma Dean*, the *Maid of the Canyon*, the *Kitty Clyde's Sister*, and the *No Name*—heavily overloaded with enough food and supplies to last the next ten months, these ten brave individuals (two of whom were added at the last minute) aspired to be the first to probe the unseen depths of the Green and Colorado Rivers as their currents raged southward through the states of Utah, Colorado, Arizona, and Nevada into the Gulf of California. The party's intended destination was a thousand miles of unexplored river downstream—a wildly ambitious and undeniably dangerous proposition, to say the least.

Aside from the legendary exploits of Lewis and Clark, the Powell expedition was the most significant and grandiose exploration into the magnificent vistas of the American West. At the time, the Colorado Plateau remained the largest unknown region of a rapidly developing America, and much of this sprawling expanse was truly *terra incognita*. Biographer William Culp

Darrah has described the Powell expedition as "the last great exploration into unknown and unmapped country in the United States." Culp also noted that, "For sheer bravery, daring, and resourcefulness, the canyon voyage had been inscribed in the annals of American exploration."

Donald Worster, in his book *A River Running West*, goes even further and boldly asserts, "Powell's journey down the legendary river of the West was one of the greatest events in the history of American exploration. Only the travels of Meriwether Lewis and William Clark some six decades earlier compare in significance or drama."

In his much-celebrated biography of Powell, *Beyond the Hundredth Meridian*, historian Wallace Stegner recognized this crowning achievement in the subtitle of his book, which says it all: *John Wesley Powell and the Second Opening of the West*. Robert Brewster Stanton aptly noted, "Whoever may have traversed the great canyons or braved the terrors of the five hundred and more cataracts and rapids of the river, it is but following that little band of '69 who blazed the way."

No one can doubt the profound significance of Powell's accomplishment. Yet, in the end, these ten adventurers were poorly prepared for the dangers that they were about to encounter. Without adequate maps, the expedition members had no way of ascertaining exactly where they were. Because they were the first to lay eyes on much of the river, which frequently fell abruptly out of sight, they never knew what foreboding obstacles might lie ahead. The men were no doubt aware they were traveling through a long series of harsh, isolated canyons marked by frequent whitewater rapids. What they could not fathom with their limited knowledge of the terrain ahead was that they were about to encounter the most intimidating rapids in all of North America. One thing was certain: Once the towering canyon walls closed in around them, there would be no easy means of escape.

Serious life-threatening hazards awaited them. Drowning in these swift currents was an obvious danger. But just as likely was the grim possibility of starving to death in the desert. If the group should have the misfortune of losing a boat—which unfortunately occurred early in the journey—the men would be severely compromised in their efforts to make it out of the canyons alive.

Even with the best equipment and boat-handling techniques, the voyage would be a truly remarkable accomplishment. Without adequate craft or accomplished skills, it would become a clawing and furious race for survival.

To make matters worse, intense personality conflicts began to take their toll. Powell's urbane and academic background contrasted sharply with the more direct and simplistic ways of the mountain men. The fact that Powell treated them like they were still enlisted in the army certainly did not help matters. Running out of food and losing valuable equipment added to the strain of the ordeal. Back-breaking portages in the vicious heat of summer sapped the last of their quickly evaporating morale.

What happened over the next 99 days was enough to dry the mouth and weaken the knees of even the most seasoned adventurer, as the 1869 Colorado River Exploring Expedition proceeded downstream through the river's magnificently sculptured canyons: Flaming Gorge, Lodore, Desolation, Gray, Stillwater, and Labyrinth Canyons on the Green River; and, after the confluence of the two rivers, Cataract, Glen, and Grand Canyons on the Colorado River.

The purpose of the expedition was at its heart a scientific one, and when the men were not battling rapids they had measurements to compile and maps to create. Malfunctioning equipment, especially the barometers, was a constant challenge, as was the task of preserving the scientific data from damage in the porous bowels of the craft they rowed downstream.

In *A River Running West*, Worster described the scientific mission of the expedition: "Whatever his digressions, Powell went into the field with system and purpose. . . . Powell had conceived of the river's exploration in the broadest possible scientific terms. He had framed a comprehensive plan of research and, for all his restless energy, had carried it out with deliberation: start with the great mountain range that tapped the clouds for snow and rain, decipher the rocks and their history, follow the drainage to lower elevations, note the variations in flora and fauna along the way, pay attention to the native people who have devised their own fashion of living in the country, move into the unknown spots on the map only when you have carefully and scientifically located them in the adjacent known."

The expedition encountered scenes of indescribable beauty— gushing waterfalls tumbling off the canyon rims into a verdant array of mosses, ferns, and flowering plants. Marble Canyon contains walls of polished gray limestone stained deep red from water oozing from oxidized formations above. Powell described the gleaming colors of the burnished canyon walls as "white, gray, pink, and purple, with saffron tints."

The incessant sun eventually broiled the men red and disintegrated their clothing, and sudden cloudbursts sent liquid mud pouring over the rims. When they finally entered the breathtaking chasm that Powell named Grand Canyon, the walls cut deeper and the rapids turned more ferocious. The river began to etch a tortured path into dark and forbidding formations of granite, and the rapids increased in size and severity. The expedition ended at Grand Wash Cliffs a little more than three months after they had begun the daunting journey. Powell's goal to become the first to navigate and plot the course of the Green and Colorado Rivers was now complete.

Powell was hailed as a hero upon his return, and his account of the expedition became a best-seller. But his own crewmembers would harshly criticize his leadership and the intense conditions he put his men through. Over the past century and a half, Powell and his biographers have managed to largely sweep such criticisms under the rug, but these provocative issues continue to be vigorously debated by whitewater boaters around campfires along the raging rivers of the American West.

More than 60 years after the 1869 expedition was over, a 1932 book titled *Colorado River Controversies*, written by Robert Brewster Stanton (who led the second successful expedition of the river), contained candid interviews with several of the original expedition members who vigorously disputed the claims of Powell. And it was more than 70 years (1947) before the complete trip diaries and reports of the other men were published by the *Utah Historical Quarterly*.

In spite of this provocative data, most biographers and historians have stuck to the fawning narrative set forth by Powell and his admirers, who have relentlessly attacked the motives and credibility of the detracting members of the expedition.

It now seems an appropriate endeavor to examine *all* the evidence surrounding the Powell expedition and its disastrous circumstances in order to draw fresh conclusions about what really happened in those dark and lonely chasms so very long ago.

PART I

BEGINNINGS

★ ★ ★ ★

CHAPTER ONE

T HE YEAR WAS 1869; THE PLACE, THE UNEXPLORED depths of the Green and Colorado Rivers; and the occasion, the ten-man Colorado River Exploring Expedition led by Major John Wesley Powell.

In the fading late-afternoon sunlight, the river's quick current shimmered like tiny, fine-cut jewels. A warm breeze nudged its way upstream through the sandstone canyon, ruffling the slender branches of the tamarisk that lined the steep, sandy shore. The faint sound of rapids rumbled downstream. The oarsmen, not knowing what dangers lay below, stood up in their wooden boats and peered cautiously into the steep walls that marked the entrance to the canyon.

The conspicuous noise downstream began, as it always does, as a low and gentle rumble. The commotion then steadily increased its pitch as frothy white waves crashed into the massive polished boulders that had fallen into the currents of the roiling, dark river.

When the exploring party reached the rapids, the roar that reverberated off the sheer canyon walls was so loud that it was like a thunderstorm beating furiously against a tin roof. The current quickened. For those inside the boats, the banks sped by so suddenly that they turned to a blur. The churning maelstrom then dropped out of sight, and an eerie mist rose from the water's surface. Tremendous danger loomed ahead.

A long, rocky ledge alongside the bank afforded a perfect vantage point for a view downstream. The men pulled the boats to shore and scurried up a large boulder scree to see the hazards that loomed below. Ten sets of eyes nervously scanned the churning water below—an explosion of water pounding violently against rock—as they searched for a route, any route, that would offer them safe passage. The pulsing maw, they eventually concluded, was likely to swallow anything even remotely exposed to it.

As the expedition closely examined the circulating current, the men observed that it was violently ripped apart, at least initially, by two large boulders. Downstream from this mayhem was a series of stair-step drops that were far worse than anything they had seen so far. Even a minor miscalculation at the top of the rapids, it was clear, would result in a boat turned upside down and pinned against a rock—or worse yet, devoured at the bottom of a recirculating wave. Either fate would prove disastrous.

It became evident that a successful negotiation of such chaos, even when negotiated by skilled boatmen, ultimately depended upon nothing more than pure luck. Should a boat catch the current at just the right point in the churning cycle, the descent could be a forgiving one on a narrow chute flowing between massive boulders. But should a boat enter at the wrong point in the churning cycle, it could be pummeled unmercifully in the trough of a vicious hole, forcing the oarsmen to pull with all their might to escape with their lives.

The stress of this stomach-wrenching unpredictability began to wear on the men as they contemplated their fate in the churning morass ahead. As someone familiar with the menacing sound of whitewater grinding its way downstream, Major Powell wrote of the harrowing experience they faced in exploring these deep and untrodden chasms:

We are now ready to start on our way down the Great Unknown. Our boats, tied to a common stake, chafe each other as they are tossed by the fretful river. They ride high and buoyant, for their loads are lighter than we could desire. We have but a month's rations remaining. The flour has been resifted through the mosquito-net sieve; the spoiled bacon has been dried and the worst of it boiled; the few pounds of dried apples have been spread in the sun and reshrunken to their normal bulk. The sugar has all melted and gone on its way down the river. But we have a large sack of coffee. The lightening of the boats has this advantage: they will ride the waves better and we shall have but little to carry when we make a portage.

We are three-quarters of a mile in the depths of the earth, and the great river shrinks into insignificance as it dashes its angry waves against the walls and cliffs that rise to the world above; the waves are but puny ripples, and we but pigmies, running up and down the sands or lost among the boulders.

We have an unknown distance yet to run, an unknown river to explore. What falls there are, we know not; what rocks beset the channel, we know not; what walls rise over the river, we know not. We may conjecture many things. The men talk as cheerfully as ever; jests are bandied about freely this morning, but to me the cheer is somber, and the jests are ghastly.

The challenging journey down the Green and Colorado Rivers is now routinely tackled by a steady stream of eager and experienced river runners in what remains one of the world's greatest whitewater adventures. Even with the latest in sophisticated equipment and river-running techniques, the journey is a serious undertaking suitable only for expert boaters with finely honed skills.

Historian Robert Brewster Stanton has said of modern-day river runners who follow in the wake of Major Powell: "The power of the current is the same, and the fall from the head to the mouth of the Grand Canyon is still as great as it was then, and the dangers of navigating a boat over and through the lashing waves of the cataracts is as great today as ever, and no skill, no experience, can enable one to foresee what a single cross-current wave may do."

The most popular whitewater craft on western rivers today is the inflatable raft, offering a number of advantages over more rigid craft. Eminently forgiving, the flexible form of the inflatable boat renders navigation of big-volume rapids relatively safe, primarily because of the craft's stability in the unpredictable waves of whitewater. The coated-fabric materials of high-quality inflatables are also surprisingly puncture-proof, and should damage occur, they are easily repaired in the field. The development of self-bailing floors makes them safer and more convenient still.

Hard-hulled dories constructed of wood, fiberglass, or aluminum are still used for battling the rapids of these rivers, but their designs are radically different from the crude wooden boats used in Powell's descent. The light weight, high sides, and symmetrical shape of the modern whitewater dory provide far greater stability and maneuverability than Powell's boats ever did. These new craft are also piloted by one person, eliminating the need for coordination among rowers.

Perhaps the greatest difference in technique between the Powell expedition and present-day whitewater boating is the direction in which the boat is rowed. Powell's men rowed in the traditional manner—downstream, with their backs to the oncoming obstacles, just as one would on a lake. Not only did this technique fail to provide a good view of the action ahead, it increased the speed at which the boat approached the river's hazards. While Jack Sumner and William Dunn rowed the *Emma Dean* with their backs to the action, Major Powell served as their eyes as he stood on deck and peered intently downstream, holding tightly onto a line attached to the bow to balance himself as he shouted orders about where they should aim the boat.

It would be years before another Colorado River boatman, Nathaniel Galloway, adopted the technique of facing forward and rowing upstream when entering the rapids. This position not only provides a better vantage point for spotting hazards downriver but utilizes the stronger muscles of the back and legs to slow the boat's speed and allow more time to maneuver around obstacles.

Powell, at the sight of boulder-filled rapids looming ahead, would have Sumner and Dunn pull the *Emma Dean* over to shore. He would walk downstream to examine the maelstrom, and then he would decide whether it was safe to risk a descent. When he found the obstacles in the river too dangerous, he adopted the conservative but tedious methods of either lining the boats with ropes alongside the banks, or taking the boats out of the water altogether and portaging them overland.

Those methods were not only time-consuming but physically difficult, and the men invariably preferred the thrill of running the rapids, just as they do today. Modern-era river runners are rarely forced to line or portage rapids, not only because detailed river maps and guidebooks (and even GPS devices) warn them of the hazards downstream but because their equipment is so much more riverworthy.

The 1869 expedition was not so fortunate. These were ten ordinary men, brave beyond measure as they entered the unknown terrain of this treacherous river, yet offering little in the way of qualifications for the monumental task of exploring the greatest whitewater rapids in the American West. The stress of not knowing where they were and of literally starving to death in the desert led four of them to mutiny the expedition, with three dying in their desperate attempt to crawl back to civilization.

The names of these ten brave individuals, those who completed the expedition and those who did not, will be forever etched into the annals of western lore:

John Wesley Powell
Walter Powell
John Coulter Sumner
George Young Bradley
William Dunn
Oramel G. Howland
Seneca Howland
William Rhodes Hawkins
Andrew Hall
Frank Goodman

CHAPTER TWO

THE MEMBERS OF THE EXPEDITION USUALLY REFERRED to Powell as the Major, even though four years had passed since he had served in the Union Army. In many ways he was a remarkable—maybe even a great—man, but most of those who signed on for the 1869 Colorado River Exploring Expedition had trouble seeing him in a light other than that of a military commander.

Perhaps his current position as a geology professor failed to offer him the same sense of destiny that the acrid smell of the Civil War battlefield did. Perhaps the tragic loss of his right arm to a musket ball at the Battle of Shiloh led to a nagging sense that he had left something significant undone. In any event, he was a strangely complicated and obsessed individual, and the men who accompanied him downriver on this dangerous undertaking came to regard him with varying degrees of admiration, respect, disdain, and utter contempt.

Two years earlier, Powell met a mountain man named Jack Sumner, who was running a mercantile store and guide service in the small resort town of Hot Sulphur Springs, Colorado. Sumner had come highly recommended, and the Major asked him to outfit a couple of scientific field trips that he was planning into the back-woods of Colorado and Utah. Powell hoped to assemble a group of former military men for outings that would map the terrain, take barometric measurements, and collect geological specimens in this remote territory. Sumner never understood why Powell insisted on recruiting those with an army background, but as he soon learned, you don't argue with the Major.

The 1867 trip started out at Plattsmouth, Nebraska, crossed the plains with mule teams to Denver, worked along the east slope of the Front Range, climbed Pikes Peak, and traveled west as far as South Park. The expedition eventually explored the headwaters of the Colorado River, which in those days was called the Grand River. The 1868 trip examined the nearby Green River and its tributaries.

After most of the group departed, Powell spent the winter of 1868 in the plateau country of western Colorado and eastern Utah with the mountain men Sumner had selected. Along with Sumner, the crew included a grizzled trapper named Bill Dunn, a fugitive from the law named Billy Hawkins, a newspaper printer named Oramel Howland, and his younger brother, Seneca.

On the banks of the White River, about a hundred miles above its junction with the Green River, the party constructed three rustic cabins for nine people to winter there—Powell, his wife Emma, his brother Walter, Sumner, Dunn, Hawkins, the Howland brothers, and a student named Sam Garman. When the weather allowed, they took long rides by mule into the desolate countryside. They explored south to the Grand River, wandered west to the Green River, and meandered north to the Uinta Mountains.

In between trips, Powell conversed with a band of Ute Indians, and he compiled a vocabulary of their language for the Smithsonian while swapping trinkets for native items that he could take back to the Illinois Natural History Museum. The winter's events were instrumental in shaping the Major's plans, and his vision soon shifted to the goal of being the first to explore the length of the Colorado River system.

Fired with this revolutionary idea, Powell returned to Chicago, where he dispatched a telegram to Sumner, asking for assistance with this epic journey to collect natural history specimens, examine the area's geology, and uncover the solution to the country's greatest remaining geographical mystery—the canyons of the Green and Colorado Rivers.

Sumner reluctantly agreed, but he pointed out the futility of beginning at the headwaters of the Grand River, which were far too rocky and dangerous to float boats of the size needed for a trip of that length, not to mention the problem of penetrating the mountainous terrain. So Powell reconsidered, and then decided to initiate the expedition at the more accessible headwaters of the Green River. The river was longer and more substantial in its flow, and most geographers believed it was, in fact, the true headwaters of the Colorado River.

In the end, the decision was one that largely turned on the logistics of transporting the boats and supplies required for such an undertaking. The railway station at Green River, Wyoming, was located along the newly constructed intercontinental railway, and the railroad company agreed to ship, at no expense, the four boats and all the necessary equipment, as well as the members of the expedition.

This was rugged country, to be sure. Not a single settlement could be found alongside the desolate river, and some of its precipitous gorges were reputed to be 5,000 feet deep. The Indians spoke of places where the river dove underground, never to resurface again. The fear of sheer waterfalls suddenly dropping hundreds of feet was on the minds of anyone who contemplated navigating these perilous gorges.

The Green River was reasonably well known from the town of Green River as far south as the Uinta River. This stretch included Flaming Gorge and Horseshoe, Kingfisher, Red, Lodore, Whirlpool, and Split Mountain Canyons.

There were widely separated pockets of the Green that were known from the Uinta Range down to Gunnison Valley (near the present town of Green River, Utah). This stretch included Desolation and Gray Canyons. But there were long, unexplored gaps below Gunnison Crossing as far south as Grand Wash Cliffs (near the present town of Meadview, Arizona). Here the knowledge of the terrain was extremely vague. This stretch included Stillwater, Labyrinth, Cataract, Glen, Marble, and Grand Canyons.

At Green River Station, Wyoming, where the expedition would begin, the elevation was 6,075 feet above sea level. Some 900 miles downstream, at Rio Virgen, Arizona, where the journey would end, the elevation was about 700 feet. The remaining mystery was how, in the course of almost a thousand miles, the river descended that vertical mile.

The Major was determined, even obsessed, with the mission of surveying the topography that lay between these two geographical points. Preparation counted for everything, and the explorers knew there would be no second chances once they departed. Their watery path would follow the Green River down to its confluence with the Grand River in Utah and continue on the Colorado River through Arizona and into the Gulf of California.

Despite Powell's military connections, the federal government viewed the exploration with some skepticism and showed no interest in sponsoring it. Powell, after all, had only led student field trips, not a true expedition, and he had only seen a small portion of the vast geographical area. Of necessity, the venture down the river became one financed largely by Powell himself.

The Powell expedition was officially conducted under the patronage of the Illinois State Historical Society, although its success later prompted other organizations to claim the honor. Initial cash contributions from other organizations were meager: Illinois State Normal University gave $500; Illinois Industrial University, $500, and the Chicago Academy of Sciences, $100. The Smithsonian provided numerous scientific instruments such as barometers and chronometers.

Congress eventually authorized a generous army order allowing the expedition to draw ten months of rations for 12 men at any western fort. Some of these rations were converted to cash. Powell spent almost $2,000 of his own money, and friends donated small sums. The Union Pacific Railroad was by far the most generous benefactor, providing the transportation for the participants, the boats, and other equipment and supplies. The ambitious Colorado River Exploring Expedition turned out to be a lean endeavor of shoestring proportions.

CHAPTER THREE

THE RIVER HAD RISEN OVERNIGHT, AND JACK
Sumner walked to its edge and threw a large piece of gray driftwood into the strong brown current. He watched it slowly flutter
before it disappeared, never to resurface again.

Weeks had passed since he and the other men arrived at the
Union Pacific depot at Green River Station, Wyoming, where
they patiently waited for the Major to arrive. Powell had made
Sumner's responsibilities as the head boatman of the expedition
clear. Joining the expedition was a voluntary endeavor for Sumner,
but at that moment it must have occurred to him that his thirst
for adventure had prevailed over common sense. Sumner hoped
the venture would make him rich and famous, but that never happened. After the dust settled, only the Major walked away from the
river a national hero.

The hamlet at Green River Station, with its hastily constructed
adobe and wooden frame buildings, had blossomed briefly, its fleet-
ing prosperity a gift from the federal government. The sleek, new
transcontinental railroad crossed the river here, bringing with it
the usual array of hucksters, prostitutes, and malcontents. But once

the tracks headed west, most of the town left with them. All that remained was a dozen dilapidated buildings, primarily wooden shacks with canvas-tarp roofs.

The expedition members stranded in this deserted shantytown had become increasingly restless, having run out of diversions. Sumner called it a "miserable adobe village." To pass the time and blunt the desolation surrounding them, the men sought solace in hard liquor and gambling, and they spent much of their time frequenting the saloon. Life was so monotonous that even the appeal of the ladies was growing thin.

Four new wooden rowboats and the mounds of food and equipment required for an expedition of this magnitude arrived at the station. Powell would be coming from Chicago with military requisitions and the scientific instruments—chronometers, barometers, sextants, thermometers, and compasses—necessary for charting unexplored territory.

Powell was unsure how long the expedition would last. He was prepared to spend ten months on the river to allow wintering over, and the expedition's food consisted of the typical rations of flour, rice, beans, coffee, and the like. As it turned out, Powell unrealistically assumed that these supplies could be augmented with plenty of fish and game that the mountain men would shoot and catch along the way.

There was some concern about the Indians. The Utes were said to be friendly, but some of the other tribes, such as the Apaches, were more hostile to the white man. Powell decided to arm everyone to the teeth, and they became walking arsenals. Each man had two revolvers, and the boats carried an additional four or five Winchester rifles, several carbines, and a number of double-barreled rifles. Each crew member also had two large hunting knives and enough ammunition for a small platoon. Hoping to pacify the

Indians, the party brought a plentiful supply of calico, tobacco, and assorted trinkets.

In the end, the expedition would last 99 days, 71 of which would actually be spent on the water.

The group was officially dubbed the Colorado River Exploring Expedition, but the name was clearly more imposing than the meager experience its members possessed. The majority of the party were mountain men, adept in the ways of hunting and trapping but completely unfamiliar with whitewater rapids like those that boiled viciously inside the deep canyons downstream. None of the men had ever run a rapid.

As lead boatman, Sumner tried to maintain a sense of discipline by having the men rise early to outfit the boats. The hungover ruffians caulked seams, secured oars, and packed the boats. They also complained bitterly about the relentless desert heat that beat down upon them in this uninspiring landscape. The food and equipment were equally divided among the three cargo boats in case one of them should be lost in a capsize.

Just before the Major's arrival at Green River Station, a man dressed in a dark suit and formal gray Stetson hat strolled into camp and introduced himself as Captain Samuel Adams. He announced to everyone that he was there to see Major Powell, explaining that he had been authorized to take command of the expedition. Needless to say, this came as something of a surprise to Sumner, who suggested that he await the Major's arrival to further discuss the matter.

Adams, who complained that he had trouble cashing a check in this desolate outpost, asked the men if he could borrow some money, and he took up a small collection. He did not remain in camp in the evenings, but returned every morning to see if the Major was there yet.

A few days later, Powell arrived at the station. His right arm amputated below the elbow, he had trouble steadying himself as he descended the steep steps of the train. He tried not to draw attention to his handicap, but it made him reliant on others, which a man of his ego resented. None of the men dared offer to help, fearing his reproach. He looked older than his 35 years, and his high forehead and piercing gray eyes overshadowed his small, five-and-a-half-foot frame.

Powell strode up to Sumner and asked to see the boats. Powell slowly circled each one, eyeing them closely. He pushed against the sides with the sole of his boot, commenting that they looked much smaller here than they did in the Chicago boatyard.

The diminutive Major, clad in clothes from his days in the military—collarless button-up muslin shirt, woolen pants, suspenders, and leather brogans—crossed the dusty street on his way to the hotel behind the saloon. The men could hear his steps echoing rhythmically on the wooden boardwalk, and they all harbored the same resentment: they had left the army, and the Major no longer owned them.

The men continued to sift through the mounds of cooking pots, blankets, guns, ammunition, oarlocks, and all the other gear needed for a journey of this magnitude. There was but one life jacket to be found among the stack of equipment, and it was reserved for the Major.

The next day Adams introduced himself to Powell, who tersely asked to see his authorization. Adams produced some vague governmental correspondence politely responding to his request for congressional approval of a journey down the river. Not impressed, the Major instructed him to leave immediately. Adams did so, never to be heard from again. Somehow in his haste to leave, he failed to repay the money he owed.

The next morning, Powell gathered the crew for breakfast around the long wooden table in the dining room of the train depot, run by a Chinese immigrant named Ah Chung, who was known for his delicious apple pies. The Major announced the expedition would leave in two weeks, and that if anyone was not up to the task, now was the time to leave. He reiterated that no alcohol would be allowed. As he gently pulled on his suspenders, he walked toward the railroad bridge that spanned the silty river.

Reaching the top of the bridge, Powell stopped and stared into the swirling current for a long time. He then slowly walked away, never looking back.

CHAPTER FOUR

THE MAJOR INTENDED TO KEEP THE PARTY SMALL. He initially invited seven others—his brother Walter, a soldier named George Bradley, and five mountaineers: Jack Sumner, Bill Dunn, Billy Hawkins, and the Howland brothers, Oramel and Seneca.

The remainder of the crew was staffed at the last minute with a couple of wild-eyed itinerants traveling through the town of Green River: an Englishman looking for adventure named Frank Goodman and a young, unemployed teamster originally from Scotland by the name of Andy Hall.

The crew assembled by Powell was undoubtedly the most eclectic collection of individuals ever brought together to undertake an exploration as perilous and momentous as this one. Seven of these men were veterans of the Civil War, which had ended four years earlier. Only Powell was formally educated and married. None of the men signed on for monetary gain. Three of them—Jack Sumner, Bill Dunn, and Oramel Howland—were paid a nominal wage for work with the sextant, barometers, and maps, but the rest of the party were volunteers. All the men, with the exception of

Bradley (why he was excluded is not known), were told they would receive $1,000 if Powell succeeded in winning governmental funding for the venture, which he never did.

Powell allowed the men to augment their pay by panning for gold and trapping for beaver and other animals. Any gold they found would be theirs, and Powell agreed to purchase pelts at specified prices.

The lure of an adventure of this magnitude was undoubtedly the primary motivation for most of the men, but they also harbored dreams of fame and fortune. Powell envisioned the journey primarily as a scientific mission to expand the knowledge of the geology, natural sciences, and ethnology of the region. But later events would make it clear that he was not averse to making a name for himself along the way.

The ten members of the expedition crowded themselves into the four craft, which were christened the *Emma Dean*, the *Maid of the Canyon*, the *Kitty Clyde's Sister*, and the *No Name*. In preparing for the expedition down the Green and Colorado Rivers, Powell decided on four craft, which would be propelled and steered by two rowers in each boat. Leading the pack was the *Emma Dean*, named after Major Powell's wife and carrying a small American flag that fluttered patriotically from its stern. Sumner, along with Dunn, rowed the *Emma Dean* with Powell on board. At Powell's request, Sumner kept a daily diary of events.

As the explorers moved downstream, Powell typically stood at the bow of the boat, allowing him to survey the hazards downstream and warn the others of the hazards that lay ahead. As a geologist, he was competent to read the strata of the canyon walls and determine what they meant for the creation of rapids that roared noisily beyond.

Sumner, the lead guide, spent a lot of time with Powell during those three months on the river (Sumner often referred to him as "the Professor"). In the process, Sumner learned much about Powell's life, beginning with the fact that his father was an itinerant Methodist minister who instilled in his son belligerent views against slavery. This controversial position placed the young Powell in constant arguments with his classmates, which no doubt strengthened his resolve. His father eventually removed him from public school and sent him to a tutor named George Crookham, who persuaded him to pursue the physical sciences and the numerous field trips that accompanied them.

Powell's father offered to pay for a seminary education, but Powell wanted no part of it. Without a college degree, he became a teacher in a one-room school. He took a few college courses in science, but most of his education came from various forays into the countryside, including several boat trips down the Ohio, Illinois, and Mississippi Rivers. He was soon elected secretary of the Illinois State Natural History Society.

The Civil War broke out when Powell was 27, and he enlisted as a volunteer officer at the rank of second lieutenant in the company led by Ulysses S. Grant. He married his second cousin, Emma Dean, in November 1861, and in April 1862 he was badly injured at the Battle of Shiloh. Two days later, with his wife at his side, his right arm was amputated below the elbow. He remained in the army until January 1865, when he resigned his commission just a few months shy of his 31st birthday.

Besides his duties as head boatman, Sumner was also responsible for the important job of taking astronomical readings with a sextant. His shots of the sun provided the numbers for calculating latitude. Longitude was determined by more complex stellar and lunar observations that were carefully timed with Powell's expensive chronometer. Once an astronomical station was established, it was then possible to determine the distance to the expedition's final destination.

The complicated scientific purpose of the expedition was a lofty one. The geographical survey was intended to chart the most important physiographic features of the canyons. Powell described the complex process of surveying and recording the landscape along the river:

> On this trip astronomic stations about fifty miles apart were made, and observations taken for latitude with the sextant, and also for longitude by the method of lunar distances. The meandering course of the river was determined by compass observations from point to point with the intervening distances estimated, thus connecting the astronomic stations. For hypsometric [height] data a series of tri-daily barometric observations were recorded, taken at the water's edge, and using this as an ever-falling base-line, altitude on the walls and such adjacent peaks as were visited were determined by synchronous observations. The results of this hypsometry [height measurement] were used in the construction of the geological sections made along the course of the river. The course of the river and the topographic features of the canyons only were mapped.

Sadly, many of the maps, field notes, and scientific journals of the expedition were accidentally lost to the river, along with a number of fossils and geological specimens.

The members of the expedition were a varied lot, but most of them originally hailed from the Northeast and Midwest. Lead boatman Jack Sumner was from Iowa, 29 years of age, and had become a hunter and trapper after serving four years in the Union

Army. He was fair-haired and delicate in appearance, but resolute in his internal constitution.

Above all else, Sumner was an avid collector of natural history specimens, and when Powell came to Hot Sulphur Springs two years earlier, he was impressed by Sumner's vast collection of animal trophies. Robert Brewster Stanton said about Sumner that he "was a true frontiersman, quiet and generous, and yet with a temper and spirit that knew no bound when he was treated unjustly by others."

Sumner remained loyal to Powell even as three of Sumner's close colleagues from Colorado (William Dunn, Oramel Howland, and Seneca Howland) deserted the venture toward its end. Sumner was the only member of the 1869 expedition whom Powell invited to join a second expedition two years later, which gives some indication of how much Powell trusted his skills and judgment.

Decades after the expedition was over, Sumner leveled severe criticisms against Powell in an interview with Stanton, claiming that Powell's lack of leadership led to the rancor that permeated the group. Incidentally, Powell also owed Sumner a fair amount of money, which was never repaid.

Manning the oars of *Emma Dean* beside Sumner was Bill Dunn, as true a mountain man as there ever was, as one could easily see by his greasy buckskins, robust beard, and long, black, braided hair. Dunn was a year older than Sumner, and he made a meager living as a trapper, hunter, and mule skinner. He was responsible for taking barometrical and altitude measurements at least three times a day at different locations.

Next among the boats came the *Maid of the Canyon*, manned by George Bradley and the Major's brother, Walter Powell. Bradley, at five foot nine and 150 pounds, was the largest and most powerful man in the party, and his substantial mustache was framed by brown hair and a dark complexion.

Bradley was raised in Newbury, Massachusetts, and had a varied background, having worked as a cobbler, druggist, and commercial fisherman. He was the only member of the expedition with any experience around boats, although he had never seen whitewater. He was a Civil War veteran and career military man who had been an orderly sergeant, and he was highly recommended to the Major by Judge William A. Carter, who owned a large mercantile in Fort Bridger, Wyoming. Powell had spent time in Fort Bridger reconnoitering the Green River, and the judge came to know Lieutenant Bradley, who had an intense fascination with the geology and fossils of the region, and who was equally eager to leave the army.

After a year of escorting Union Pacific Railroad construction crews and guarding the overland stage route, Bradley said he would "gladly explore the River Styx" to be released from his military obligations. In return for his promise to join the expedition, Powell took care of Bradley's military obligations, and just ten days before the expedition shoved off, Bradley was discharged by special order of the Secretary of War.

Powell described Bradley in the official trip report: "He was scrupulously careful, and a little mishap worked him into a passion; when labor was needed he had a ready hand, and in danger, rapid judgment and unerring skill. A great difficulty or peril changed the petulant spirit into a brave and generous soul." Bradley would later save the Major's life not once, but twice, when he rescued him from the roiling and treacherous currents of the river.

Bradley secretly kept a diary that was unknown to Powell. Its frank assessment of the situation on the river renders it the most candid record of the expedition. William Culp Darrah described the diary this way: "It is written in literary style, and despite the brevity of many of the entries, they are sensitively suggestive of the temper of the men and the river." Darrah also said that it was "by far the most important diary of the expedition."

The Major's younger brother, Walter Powell, who was 33 and two years younger than the Major, rowed the *Maid of the Canyon* beside Bradley. Also known as "Captain," he was an extremely sullen and ill-tempered individual, and he exhibited a disturbing mental illness. He could, on occasion, exhibit quite a temper, especially if he felt his brother's reputation was at stake. Most of his psychological problems no doubt resulted from his ten-month captivity by the Confederate Army during the war.

One of the members of the expedition, Bill Hawkins, later remarked about Walter Powell: "We all considered the Captain demented because of his imprisonment in Andersonville Prison. Had it not been for this, I doubt very much if the Captain would have made the entire trip." Walter largely kept to himself on the river, but at night he used his fine bass voice and repertoire of hymns and ballads to entertain the men around the campfire.

Then there was the *Kitty Clyde's Sister*, named after a popular song of the time and manned by Billy Hawkins and Andy Hall. In his diary, Sumner said, referring to those two individuals, that the *Kitty Clyde's Sister* was "manned by as jolly a brace of boys as ever swung a whip over a lay ox." Curiously enough, Hawkins on occasion went by the curious pseudonym of Billy Rhodes, presumably to evade the long arm of the law. He apparently had a checkered criminal past that was never completely revealed.

Hawkins was without a doubt the most colorful member of the party. In his mid-20s, he was admired by the others for his irrepressible spirit. He could be depended upon for anything and under the most adverse circumstances. He served cheerfully as the expedition cook, for which he received a small stipend. When meals were ready, he yelled out in true bullwhacker style, "Plunder!

Plunder! Come and get it!" It was a call the men fondly recalled years later, when the expedition was but a distant memory.

Hawkins's later interviews about the journey were extremely critical of Powell, who owed, but never repaid, Hawkins significant sums for wages, horses, and other equipment sold to the expedition. In spite of this animosity, Hawkins, along with Sumner and three others (Walter Powell, George Bradley, and Andy Hall), continued on with Powell until the bitter end.

Crew member Andy Hall, who rowed *Kitty Clyde's Sister* along with Hawkins, had immigrated to Illinois from Scotland as a young boy, later working as an Indian scout on wagon trains that hauled freight across the prairies of the West. Only 19 years of age, he was the youngest member of the expedition. He had been loitering around Green River Station when Powell quickly spotted him, with his long hair and prominent beak of a nose. Andy remained good-natured under the worst circumstances, a trait that served the expedition members well as they inched their way downstream during the grueling three months on the river.

Bringing up the rear of the party was the *No Name*, manned by the Howland brothers and Frank Goodman. Oramel Howland, the elder brother, was well spoken and worked as a printer and editor for the *Rocky Mountain News*. At 36, he was the oldest member of the party. He was raised in Vermont and ventured out West, where he eventually made his home in Colorado. Powell remarked in his writings that when the wind whipped through Oramel's long hair and massive beard, he had "a wild look, much like that of King Lear in an illustrated copy of Shakespeare."

Oramel was by all accounts a quiet and gentle character. His official job on the expedition, for which he was compensated, was the important one of producing topographical renderings of the river. Each time the party rounded a point, Howland noted the compass direction and estimated the distance to the next point. Along with Dunn's elevations, the resulting figures produced a constantly descending baseline from which triangulations could be made for estimating the height of the canyon walls. The river map that resulted was then placed on broader maps of the area.

Oramel's younger brother, Seneca, was just 26, and he moved West at his brother's repeated insistence. Seneca had been injured at Gettysburg, and he generally stayed clear of the personality conflicts that plagued the group.

Rounding out the crew, and joining the Howland brothers in the *No Name*, was Frank Goodman, a young, red-faced Englishman searching for western adventure. He was so eager to join the expedition that it has been speculated he offered to pay Powell for the privilege. Whether Powell accepted the money, if it was offered, no one knows for sure.

None of the men, it was clear from the beginning, had any significant experience around boats or waterways before joining the expedition. Powell relied on the mountain men to supplement the pantry with wild game, but they soon discovered that a barren desert makes for slim hunting grounds. It was inevitable that dissension would erupt among such a diverse assortment of individuals on such a wildly dangerous venture as this. Looking back at the scope and magnitude of the undertaking, it is amazing that Powell could hold the expedition together long enough to fulfill his ambition as the first descent of the Colorado River system.

It is a true testament to Powell's peculiar fitness for the formidable task set before him. But the acrimony among the crew took a heavy toll on the lives of those who had joined the Major on this historic quest of one of the world's most dangerous rivers.

CHAPTER FIVE

THE MAJOR, BY ALL ACCOUNTS, WAS COMPLETELY undaunted by the prospect that the expedition would be entering a huge swath of the Southwest that had never been charted before. With the exception of scattered and largely unreliable reports by Indian scouts, most of these expanses, especially those farther downstream, were unknown. Maps of the day simply stenciled the forbidding term UNEXPLORED across its vast blank spaces.

In his official report, Powell referred to the region simply as "The Great Unknown." As a geologist, he had a general idea of the lay of the land. He knew the headwaters of the Green and Colorado Rivers arose in the craggy 13,000- and 14,000-foot heights of the Rocky, Wind River, Uinta, and Wasatch Ranges of Colorado, Wyoming, and Utah. He was generally aware that the waters of the two rivers made their way into the vast Colorado Plateau, where they merged before winding a tortured and rambunctious path to the sea in the Gulf of California. But that is about all he knew.

The Major's immediate interest was focused on the Green

River, which was known to the local Crow and Shoshone Indians as the Prairie Hen River. Powell had seen it spring forth as a
trickle beneath the granite crags of central Wyoming, where its rivulets gradually gather tributaries and become a substantial stream
emerging on the southern plains of Wyoming. Here the expedition
would begin its historic journey.

Downstream, the river enters Utah and then, ever so briefly,
the northwest corner of Colorado as it bends sharply around the
massive bulwark of the east-west-trending Uinta Mountains and
into the 3,000-foot gorges that gave the expedition a tremendous
amount of grief in its first two weeks on the river.

Continuing to flow south, the Green River pierces Utah's
rugged Tavaputs Plateau and the San Rafael Valley before its even-
tual confluence with the Grand River to become the Colorado
River. Powell was well aware that in its meandering course the
Green dropped a significant distance—9,000 feet in 700 miles.

Then came the true *terra incognita*. Downstream from its
juncture with the Green, the Colorado enters a series of stark
and majestic chasms that Powell named Cataract Canyon, Glen
Canyon, and Grand Canyon. It was here that the expedition faced
the largest and most intimidating rapids.

Powell yearned to be the first to ply these unseen depths and
to discover the scientific secrets that lay therein. But despite his
exhaustive efforts, he met great resistance in his efforts to obtain
government sponsorship. As a result, he was forced to finance
much of the expedition from his own meager funds, not the generous grants the federal government had disbursed to Lewis and
Clark 65 years earlier.

The boats that Powell had custom built for the descent were
clearly inadequate for the task. They were far better suited for
rowing the placid waters of lakes than dodging the rapids of

rock-infested rivers. The boats featured low sides, rounded hulls, and pronounced keels, and these characteristics rendered them somewhat unwieldy and prone to tipping.

These were hardly the ideal craft with which to negotiate the boisterous currents of whitewater. Three of the four boats were constructed with double planks of cured oak, which made them extremely durable but also extraordinarily heavy.

Boats and supplies weighing thousands of pounds posed a significant dilemma. Powell anticipated that the journey might require wintering over, so he was careful to pack enough provisions for ten months, even though he believed the journey most likely would not take half that time. A prolonged outing like this required significant stores of food, guns, ammunition, and tools for building winter shelters. This substantial weight slowed the party's progress even further. The expedition eventually required about a hundred days to complete its mission, and the albatross of behemoth boats nearly killed them.

Powell had initially considered constructing the boats at the edge of the river's headwaters. But as he became more familiar with the swift, rock-studded streams of the Rockies, Powell realized that no ordinary boat could withstand the intense pounding of rocks and whitewater. He traveled to Chicago in February 1869 to meet with the well-known boat maker, Thomas Bagley. There, on the north end of the Clark Street Bridge, he ordered four boats made to his specifications for the journey into the dark and unknown canyons.

Three of the boats were of the same dimensions: 21 feet long, 4 feet wide, and 2 feet deep. Built of oak and double ribbed with wine-glass transoms, they were exceptionally stout and designed to withstand significant stress. The boats were divided into 5-foot-long bow and stern compartments for storage of gear and to add buoyancy in case of capsize. The fourth boat was considerably smaller—16 feet long and 4 feet wide—and constructed of a more fragile pine. It was lighter and more maneuverable to serve as the lead boat, and it did not contain internal compartments.

The boats resembled ferry tenders that plied the Chicago River and Lake Michigan, so they rode deeply in the water. They performed efficiently on flat water, but were not well suited for whitewater.

First of all, they were too long and narrow to be very maneuverable. Second, they were shallow and prone to shipping water. Third, with rounded bottoms they tended to be unstable in waves. Last, their weight rendered them exceptionally slow in response to the oars.

The water that entered the boats had to be laboriously bailed out by hand with camp kettles. Because the boats were large enough to hold hundreds of gallons of water (weighing about eight pounds a gallon), they became even more cumbersome after running even the mildest rapids, which often filled them to the brim.

The oarsmen soon learned the inviolate rule of the river: a heavy boat is always an unwieldy boat. The incredible amount of food and supplies necessary for a journey of this duration was divided among the three large boats in case one of them should be lost to the river. The smaller and lighter *Emma Dean* carried only a few scientific instruments, some clothing, and several guns.

The crew rowed the boats in the traditional manner, with the bows pointed downstream, so that the rowers' backs were to the obstacles. In hindsight, this was a remarkable mistake. Not only did this position fail to provide a good view of the action ahead, it increased the boats' speed, with obstacles oncoming, which was not an advantage in current as swift as this.

The men came to enjoy running the rapids, rendering them among the first recreational whitewater boaters in history. In his diary, George Bradley expressed their enthusiasm:

> *The rapid we started with this morning gave us to understand the character of the day's run. It was a wild one. The boats labored hard but came out all right. The waves were frightful and had any of the boats shipped a sea it would have been her last for there was no still water below. We ran a wild race for about two miles, first pulling right—then left, now to avoid the waves and now to escape the boulders, sometimes half full of water and as soon as a little could be thrown out it was replaced by double the quantity.*

To negotiate the river hazards downstream, Powell developed a disciplined method of approach. The three boats following the Major were ordered to stay 100 yards apart. Powell developed a system of flag signals to be displayed from the bow of the *Emma Dean*: a flag waved to the right or left meant the boats should move in that direction, and a flag moved down meant "Land at once."

At the sight of substantial rapids, Powell instructed Sumner and Dunn to pull to shore. Powell, either alone or with Sumner and Bradley, would walk downstream to examine the obstacles that littered the current. Powell then made the decision of whether to risk a descent. When he found the rapids too dangerous, he took the seemingly safer alternative of either lining the boats with ropes along the shore or taking the boats out of the water and carrying them overland. Those techniques were not only time-consuming and tedious, but sometimes just as dangerous as running the rapids themselves.

The arduous process of lining and portaging the boats caused no small amount of grumbling by the men. They preferred the thrill and excitement of running the rapids to the painful drudgery of moving around them. The diary notes of Bradley revealed their disdain for lining and portaging:

> *Have been working like galley slaves all day. Have lowered the boats all the way with ropes and once unloaded and carried the goods around one very bad place. The rapid is continuous and not improving. Where we are tonight it roars and foams like a wild beast.*

The scenario of moving the boats around boulders and rapids would repeat itself scores of times before the expedition was over.

PART II

FLAMING GORGE, LODORE, AND WHIRLPOOL CANYONS

DAYS 1–33: MAY 24–JUNE 25

★ ★ ★ ★

BRIEF TIMELINE

May 26: Flaming Gorge
June 9: Disaster Falls
June 17: Fire in Camp
June 21: Whirlpool Canyon

CHAPTER SIX

IT WAS SHORTLY AFTER NOON ON MONDAY, MAY 24, 1869, when the Colorado River Exploring Expedition finally pushed off from the shores of Green River Station, Wyoming, after a month of preparations in this desolate outpost. Major Powell wrote:

> *We are quite proud of our little fleet as it lies in the river, waiting for us to embark; the stars and stripes, spread by a stiff breeze, over the* Emma Dean, *the waves rocking the little vessels, and the current of the Green River, swollen, mad and seeming eager to bear us down through its mysterious canyons. And we are just as eager to start.*

The adventurers, most of whom were hungover from a late night on the town, let out a few celebratory shouts to the handful of locals gathered on the bank to see them off.

As the explorers were whisked through the bluffs and buttes of shale in shades of dull gray, brown, and light green, they glanced over their shoulders to catch their last glimpse of civilization, for how long they did not know. The boats disappeared from view, and the crowd quietly dispersed, not particularly optimistic that the men they had briefly come to know would ever be seen alive again.

Their departure, it is safe to say, was hardly an auspicious one. The crew was not familiar with either the hydraulics of river currents or the handling of boats, and these glaring inadequacies quickly revealed themselves. Three oars were lost to the river on the first day. This could not be considered a positive omen.

The Major erroneously assumed that because the men had spent years in the mountains, they could easily adapt to the ways of the river. The transition from land to water was much more difficult than any of them anticipated, and the crew was well aware that they would soon be entering canyons full of whitewater.

The three large boats—*Maid of the Canyon*, *Kitty Clyde's Sister*, and *No Name*—were overloaded with supplies, and the boats were slow to respond to the pull of the oars. Stored within each of the large craft was 2,000 pounds of cargo stashed away in the watertight bulkheads at each end.

Only a mile or two from their departure at Green River Station, Hawkins the cook and Hall the Scotsman, rowing *Kitty Clyde's Sister*, ground the boat firmly on a sandbar in the middle of the muddy river. To dislodge it, the men jumped out and pushed with all their might. The situation repeated itself a few miles downstream, and the other men let out a barrage of friendly chastisement.

For all the levity, the next error in judgment proved disastrous. Repeated groundings continued to frustrate Hawkins and Hall, and they concluded that the problem was too much weight in the boat. Their solution, which seemed reasonable at the time, was to lighten the load. So they proceeded to dump 500 pounds of bacon into the river. When the men later struggled against starvation, that spectacular act of stupidity would come to haunt them.

Dunn the mountain man expressed his thoughts about the chances of the party's success: "If we fail, it will be due to our lack of judgment. If we succeed, it will be because of dumb luck."

The group made ten miles the first day before stopping for the evening in a lovely grove of cottonwoods. The oarsmen had trouble reading the hazards in the silt-laden current, particularly the eddies, which frustrated them by carrying the boats back upstream.

That evening the party landed the boats far downstream from the spot Powell chose. The men disembarked from the boats and pulled back upstream to the campsite. Powell stared down on the men while they struggled with the boats. He was not amused.

The expedition set up camp underneath an overhanging cliff near a steep talus slope of rock and sand. Here the gray and tan landscape was broken only by a few scattered cottonwoods, box elders, and sagebrush. There was much work to be done, and the men performed their duties.

Sumner the lead boatman took a number of sextant readings. Dunn the mountain man and Oramel Howland the printer hunted for wild game, but they came back with only a small rabbit. Sumner remarked that it was "rather slim rations for ten hungry men."

The Powell brothers and Bradley the soldier struck off for several hours in search of rocks and fossils. They managed to get lost on their way back, which is not difficult to do in such terrain. The three of them stumbled back into camp as the sun was setting. Powell later wrote:

Standing on a high point, I can look off in every direction over a vast landscape, with salient rocks and cliffs glittering in the evening sun. Dark shadows are settling in the valleys and gulches, and the heights are made higher, and the depths deeper by the glamour and witchery of light and shade. Away

*to the south, the Uinta Mountains stretch in a long line; high
peaks thrust into the sky, and snow fields glittering like lakes of
molten silver; and pine forests in somber green; and rosy clouds
playing around the borders of huge black masses; and heights
and clouds and mountains and snow fields and forest and rock-
lands are blended into one grand view.*

Beneath a full moon, Hawkins prepared a large pot of deer
stew and potatoes, and the men lined up with tin plates to receive
their share of the meal. Hawkins instinctively washed Powell's left
hand in preparation for dinner, as he had done the previous two
summers. The crew ate voraciously, and the meal was proclaimed a
grand success.

There was, however, a noticeable omission to an otherwise perfect dinner. Powell forbade liquor, and after weeks of carousing in
Green River Station, the men missed their evening drink. Sumner
reported, "We turned in early, as most of the men had been up several preceding nights, taking leave of their many friends, 'a la Mus-
covite.' The natural consequences were foggy ideas and snarly hair."

Powell ate apart from the group, which set a bad precedent for
collegiality. When the dishes were washed, he bade everyone good-
night and walked off into the darkness to find a place in the sand to
sleep. His brother Walter quietly followed. The rest of the group sat
around the campfire and took turns in coarse jesting and tall tales.
The light from the flames danced wildly on the pale canyon walls.

The men talked about things they knew best—big-game hunting in Colorado and the killing fields of the Civil War. Bradley
reminisced about all the beautiful women in Green River Station.
Hall countered in jest, with his Scottish accent, that perhaps Bradley's memory had gone bad.

On a more serious note, Sumner made clear that if the group

was to survive, they had better learn how to handle the boats before they met the whitewater downstream. Dunn, clad in his filthy buckskins, likened maneuvering the boats to pushing a wheelbarrow of bricks uphill. Everyone agreed that the two men trying to control a single boat just made matters more complicated.

Exhausted at the end of the day, the men laid down on the ground in their damp clothes, most of them government issued from their time in the military. Their only covering for the cool night was a thin wool blanket and a canvas tarp.

The second day out, the expedition was on the river early. Powell was determined to run the expedition like a military maneuver, and he wanted to be moving by six o'clock and on the river shortly thereafter. There was no small amount of grousing among the men about the early hour of departure. They had been discharged from the army and were not eager to return to its rigid structure. Hawkins served a big breakfast of ham, hash browns, and black coffee. The explorers finished packing the boats and shoved off.

As Sumner and Dunn rowed the *Emma Dean* into the current, Powell warned the others not to pass him under any circumstance. He reminded them that when he gave the signal to pull over, it should be executed immediately. The Major predicted the current would start picking up speed and there would be little time to get to shore.

The Green River in these first 60 miles is a mild stream, meandering through an evocative landscape of arid clay hills, broken badlands, and sweeping flats of sagebrush. Aprons of silt obstruct the current, and by midmorning the men were dripping wet from jumping out of the boats to dislodge them from sandbars. A barrage of foul words quickly followed the familiar sound of a boat scraping against gravel before it came to an abrupt stop. To make matters worse, it started to rain.

After a brief stop on shore, Hawkins bagged a nice lunch after stumbling across a young mountain sheep sleeping on a ledge. He killed the sheep by throwing it off the cliff. Hall joked that perhaps the animal was already dead, but no one complained about the meal served a few hours later.

Meanwhile, Powell and Bradley climbed to the canyon rim to take a number of scientific measurements and to watch the river wind its tortured path through the narrow chasm. Powell seemed pleased with the group's progress so far.

It rained for several days after, and the men continued their usual afternoon routines. Almost everyone had a painful skin condition arising from a combination of the moisture and sand while rowing. Sand was everywhere—in the boats, their clothes, the food—and avoiding it was impossible. The only relief from the grinding tedium was frequent stops to build fires to dry out and make coffee, also filled with sand.

When the group pulled into shore at night, the geologists searched for fossils scattered among the buttes, bluffs, and pinnacles of sandstone and shale, arrayed in strata of gray and buff, red and brown, and blue and black, many of which had been eroded into strange and exotic shapes. The hunters pursued sheep, beaver, geese, and anything else they could find. At this point the boats carried plenty of staples (flour, sugar, coffee, beans, and dried apples), but Powell reminded them that they needed fresh meat every few days to survive.

The party eventually arrived at Henry's Fork, a full-throated tributary entering from the west. They had traveled 60 miles from Green River Station in four days. Here the party dug up a trove of provisions and scientific instruments—chronometers, barometers, and sextants—that were cached here the previous year. The men spent several days taking scientific observations.

The crew's eyes slowly followed the canyon walls as they soared overhead. Bradley writes:

Tis the grandest scenery I have found in the mountains and I am delighted with it. I went out to see the country this morning and found it grand beyond conception.

At night the party camped on a broad sandbar full of sagebrush, which jutted into the fast-flowing river. The men sat around a campfire, entertained by Walter Powell's fine baritone voice singing gospel hymns. As they gazed at the narrow swath of sky between the canyon walls and into a dark void filled with stars close enough to touch, the rest of the world seemed very far away indeed.

The next few days, the shore consisted of arid, gravelly hills accentuated by huge buttes and cliffs rising against a clear sky of deep blue sapphire. A brisk wind tore across the bleak terrain. The nearest Mormon settlement was a hundred miles to the west, and it was twice that distance to any sign of civilization to the east.

The wind blew, and the men were finally able to get a fire started. Hawkins cooked a slab of bacon and a batch of biscuits smothered in grease, and everyone declared it a success. The men consumed endless cups of coffee dipped from the tin kettle. They had no idea how much they would miss these breakfasts when they later ran precariously low on food.

The nights were cold, and the men huddled around the fire to stay warm and cheer each other on. For supper every night they feasted on bacon, sourdough bread, and beans. They packed a large supply of tobacco for trading with the Indians, and soon their own pipes were burning. To make their blankets go farther, they often bunked together in pairs.

That night they stared into the marvelous star-filled sky, and it took some time before they got to sleep. The fire flickered out, and the men slept soundly beside the quiet stream.

The next several days the countryside was more broken, and there was a multitude of cliffs, buttes, and mesas. At times they traveled through high rocky banks, and at other times a valley several miles wide. The keels of the boats constantly grated against the bottom of the riverbed, and the men jumped overboard to lighten the load and to pull the boats into deeper current.

In the rapids the boats easily shipped water and the men remained constantly wet. Each had two sets of clothes, one for the river and the other for camp. They were spread out each night on the rocks to dry, but the next morning the men complained about putting on cotton and wool clothing that was still damp with the dew that fell overnight.

CHAPTER SEVEN

AHEAD OF THE EXPEDITION FOR THE NEXT SEVERAL days were four short but spectacular canyons: Flaming Gorge, Horseshoe Canyon, Kingfisher Canyon, and Red Canyon. The men relaxed and absorbed the beauty of their quiet depths and successfully negotiated the gentle stretches of whitewater laid out before them.

The snowy line of the ragged Uinta Range stretched from west to east across the horizon of northern Utah, adding a touch of alpine splendor to an otherwise barren array of bluff-colored cliffs and buttes. Stands of pine, spruce, aspen, and alder contrasted sharply with the walls of eroded sandstone. This majestic profile of mountains was still miles away, but the sky was so clear that the peaks seemed to be on top of the expedition.

In the distance the men could see the brilliant red rocks that marked the entrance to the first major canyon. As the party neared the chasm, its imposing 1,000-foot-high jaws glowed in the fading sunlight like a burning orb. Powell described the monolith ahead:

At a distance of from one to twenty miles a brilliant red gorge
is seen, the red being surrounded by broad bands of mottled
buff and gray at the summit of the cliffs, and curving down
to the water's edge on the nearer slope of the mountain. This
is where the river enters the mountain range—the head
of the first canyon we are to explore . . . We have named it
"Flaming Gorge."

The explorers entered the beautiful corridor of vermillion whose walls were separated by bands of mottled buff and gray. The river's banks were lined with tall cottonwood trees, whose gray-green leaves flickered resplendently against the red rocks. The party set up camp at the entrance of the canyon.

Viewed from above, the scene below—the steeply inclined walls of the canyon, rising sharply from the water's edge in graceful curves; the boats, their lines tugging gently against the pulsing current; the campfire, with smoke whirling upward in the wind; and the men, scurrying about in their chores—was a cozy one in the fading sunlight. The party expected to be enclosed within these depths for the next several days.

The expedition, as usual, took an array of barometrical observations. These revealed that they had descended 250 feet from Green River Station, which, as the crow flies, was only about 60 miles away. The men continued to pinpoint their geographical location in order to check the work of the topographers.

A mercurial barometer was read three times a day, and aneroid barometers were checked for comparison with the mercurial instruments. The tubes of mercury often broke, and new ones had to be boiled to replace them. This tedious and time-consuming process proved to be endless trouble. The wind was constantly blowing, and windscreens had to be constructed to keep the alcohol stove from going out.

Whenever possible, the men climbed out of the canyon in every direction, mostly because it offered grandiose views of the river below and the mountain peaks above. It also aided in determining their precise location.

The leisurely camps beneath the cottonwood were memorable ones. The men recorded their thoughts on paper, washed dishes, cleaned guns, mended and laundered clothes, and otherwise organized the gear. Ensconced between perpendicular cliffs of limestone, the men noted in their diaries how overwhelmed they were by the natural beauty around them.

The next day the river suddenly changed its mood. The current surged, and the men noticed something ominous about its startling force. They soon beheld their first significant rapid, gleaming like a jewel in the sunlight that pierced the narrow gorge. The rapid was swift and straightforward, and it would have hardly been worth mentioning had it not been the point where the river signaled the first of hundreds of rapids to come.

By noon the men emerged into a wider and more broken canyon. For lunch, they walked to the mouth of a crystal-clear creek that was verdant with trees and bushes. The air was full of kingfishers darting about, and the scenery was so enticing they spent the rest of the day there.

The walls of the chasm rose higher the next morning. One canyon melded into the next, and the expedition camped in a thick grove of cottonwoods. When they shoved off the next day, they heard in the distance a steady roar, but one with more sinister overtones. They were clearly nearing something of a greater magnitude, and the Major was concerned about the consequences of losing a boat.

The vertical walls soared straight toward the heavens, and the expedition spent the morning negotiating sharp turns in the river. That afternoon they ran several small drops before arriving at a long descent that required careful observation from the shore.

The river here was a hundred yards wide, and the thrashing waves were more than five feet high. The current broke upstream as it swept over finely polished boulders. The smooth cliffs, beautifully sculpted, now rose to 1,500 feet.

After closely studying the rapids, the group decided to unload the boats and line them around the drop before darkness fell. When they finished, a smooth beach of sand dotted with willows offered a pleasant camp. Dinner was prepared, and Hawkins loudly announced its arrival in typical style: "Roll out, bulls in the corral, chain up the gaps!"

The descent the next day was a nearly continuous one, with sudden drops thrown in for good measure. The party was growing proficient at bailing water out of the boats. A routine of sorts developed: The oarsmen heard a dull roar, and they hugged the bank before proceeding cautiously to the head of the rapids. An immense rock appeared in the middle of the river, and the current veered sharply around it. The swift chutes on either side were often clear, but if not—and the cataract was too risky to run—they portaged around it.

On many occasions, the banks of the river contained a mass of boulders where it was impossible to portage a boat. The men cleared a trail to a bench above the rapids, and then pushed the boats on top of log skids to a landing below. The cargo was then carried downstream.

The men by now were completely spent, the sun was beginning to set, and it was too late to do anything but pull over. A small level spot among the rocks had to serve as the evening's camp. The brilliant moonlight hung over the canyon and lit up the river, just as the mist rose from its purling surface.

As the expedition moved downstream, the drop of the river became more pronounced. These were the most violent rapids the expedition had encountered so far, and the waves tossed the heavy boats around like leaves before a storm.

The massive red slabs of sandstone, now 2,500 feet high, were arrayed almost perpendicularly to the river. In the secluded grottoes along the shore there was surprisingly luxurious vegetation—pine, spruce, cottonwood, aspen, and alder.

Late in the afternoon, the expedition emerged into a small valley hemmed in by rounded mountains. Camp was pitched under several large pine trees, and the men used the brief respite to patch the boats and to wash clothes. Several of them climbed to a high vantage point to take measurements. The splendidly panoramic view also allowed them to trace the river as it throbbed through the deep gorges in the distance.

The expedition spent a day studying geology and topography, climbing the canyon walls, compiling notes of their observations, making repairs to the boats, and a host of other duties. The expedition left the area with great regret, and plunged into half a dozen rapids before entering a wide valley. The evening's camp was pitched beneath the shade of an old cottonwood, and the explorers enjoyed the accomplishment of having put 25 miles of canyon behind them.

The next day the river took a hard right, with a deep canyon entering in from river left. Raging flash floods had swept huge boulders and uprooted trees into the main channel, forcing the quickening current against sheer cliffs on the opposite side. The boulders at the entry of the rapids were easy to spot, but everything else—beyond the brink—was out of sight. The men knew that running the rapids would be a complete shot in the dark.

The oarsmen rowed the boats to the right shore to take a closer look, but they realized they had landed on the wrong side of the river. They were now frightfully close to the lip of the rapids, and they feared the boats would be sucked into its roaring maw.

Crossing the river was impossible with the larger boats full of gear. To solve the dilemma, Sumner and Dunn rowed the nimbler *Emma Dean*, full of cargo from the other boats, to the opposite shore. Even this simple maneuver was precarious because of the peaceful draw of the current. The men stroked furiously on the oars to avoid being pulled into the cataract, and they made it to the other bank with only feet to spare.

The rest of the day the *Emma Dean* was used for shuttling the thousands of pounds of supplies across the river, and on each crossing the boat inched precariously close to the hole that roared downstream.

After the gear was transported, the portage of the boats began. Moving heavy boats on slippery rocks was a difficult endeavor, resulting in many battered legs and pinched hands. The arduous task in the stifling heat went on late into the night. The crew was completely spent by the early morning hours, and they collapsed to catch a few hours of sleep before continuing.

The next morning the men proceeded down the river, now almost as placid as a pond. There were two short canyons with walls sculpted of blood-red sandstone several hundred feet high. Thousands of swallows swarmed there, and the river, dotted with islands, began to widen. The crew, having spent a week battling rapids, indulged in the casual pace the river now thankfully afforded them.

CHAPTER EIGHT

THE MAJOR'S METHODOLOGY FOR RUNNING WHITE-
water was a fairly straightforward yet highly practical one. The
lighter and more maneuverable lead boat, the *Emma Dean*, went
in advance of the others, which closely followed in strict obedience
to the Major's signals.

The Major stood on the front deck, staring intently downstream to examine the rapids' features—known in today's whitewater parlance as "reading the water." Sumner and Dunn stopped
rowing and allowed the boat to drift.

If Powell could see a clear chute between the rocks, he
ordered the rowers to enter the cataclysm. If the channel was
obstructed, he signaled the other boats to pull to shore while he
jumped out and walked along the banks for a closer look at the
hazards below.

When the current was littered with boulders that had been
thrust into the river by flash floods from side streams or had fallen
from the canyon walls, the Major ordered the men to begin lining
or portaging the rapids. He was determined not to lose a single
boat, which would compromise the group's chances of escaping the

canyon alive. "We have enough to worry about without losing a boat," he warned the crew.

The men pulled the boats to the head of the rapids and either coaxed them alongside the shore with lines attached or made an arduous portage of boats and supplies over the rocks. Sumner commented, "Then came the real hard work, carrying the freight a hundred yards or more over a mass of loose rocks, tumbled together like the ruins of some old fortress. Not a very good road to pack seven thousand pounds of freight."

The men complained about Powell's overly cautious and, to their minds, fearful attitude toward the rapids. They soon detested the miserable work of moving the boats around the rapids. The routine was not only tedious, but surprisingly dangerous. All the supplies had to first be removed from the boat and manually carried alongside the bank to the quiet water below. Each boat was equipped with a thick hemp rope that was 100 feet in length. The rope was secured to the bow and then unfurled downstream and tied to a large boulder or tree, which served as a kind of tether should the stern line break free.

Several men then grabbed the stern line and lowered the boat downriver a few feet at a time, while those along the banks or inside the boat kept it in the water and away from the shoreline. If the boat was caught on a rock in the river, the men waded out into the water, where they were careful not to be swept off their feet by the strong current.

Once the length of the stern rope was exhausted, the bowline had to be reeled in to bring the boat back to the bank. This was a strenuous and tricky maneuver, and rope-burned hands were common for those trying to subdue the wildly bucking beast of a boat.

Even more exhausting was the situation where a rapid would

not allow lining and the boats had to be lifted out of the water and carried along the rocky banks to quiet water below. This dilemma was compounded by the boulder-filled shoreline. Carrying a 2,000-pound, 20-foot-long boat in the heat of summer over slippery rocks was, to put it mildly, an arduous task.

As the party proceeded downriver, the canyon walls narrowed in width and soared in height. This was an abrupt and magnificent gateway to the canyon, and it was obvious that severe rapids would soon follow. Sumner looked over his shoulder and warned, "Here she goes, boys. We'll have our share of trouble today." Dunn yelled to the others to tie everything down in case the boats capsized. The Major edged closer to the bow of the boat and peered intently downstream. Sun streamed into the canyon with a dazzling brilliancy.

Lapping vigorously against the sides of the boats, the waves increased in size, and soon the boats were rocking rambunctiously from side to side. The oarsmen instinctively stopped rowing. The churning noise grew louder and then deepened in pitch. Large boulders littered the streambed, and the river made an abrupt turn to the right. The expedition nervously rounded the blind corner. All the men could see ahead were the tops of waves thrashing about and foam being thrown into the air.

The members of the expedition had to shout to one another to be heard above the roar. The Major gave a hand signal indicating the need to close up the formation of boats. "We may be in for some trouble here," Powell warned as he tightened his grip on the rope with his one good hand.

The powerful current grabbed the *Emma Dean* and yanked her downstream with a startling force. Sumner and Dunn pulled powerfully on the oars, doing everything they could to keep the bow pointed directly into the waves, where the craft would be more stable and less likely to capsize. The boat pitched violently from front to rear, and then from side to side, and the Major kneeled on the floor to avoid being tossed overboard.

Sumner and Dunn managed to thread the needle through massive boulders and deep pourovers in a current that churned downstream with astonishing speed. The run was over almost as quickly as it began. The men furiously bailed out the water that had filled the boat to the gunnels. Sumner gleefully recounted:

> The Emma *being very light is tossed about in a way that threatens to shake her to pieces, and is nearly as hard to ride as a Mexican pony. We plunge along, singing, yelling, like drunken sailors, all feeling that such rides do not come every day. It was like sparking a black-eyed girl—just dangerous enough to be exciting.*

The other three boats followed closely in the wake of the *Emma Dean*. One moment they were climbing steep waves, with foaming crests pouring over them, and the next minute they were plunging straightforward into deep troughs that seemed to go on forever.

The *Maid of the Canyon* at one point veered sideways into the current and began to tip over. Bradley and Walter Powell braced themselves for the inevitable capsize, but at that very moment a powerful wave hit the boat from the opposite side and suddenly righted them.

When they reached the quiet water below, the two men were stunned at their good fortune, and they shouted with glee as they stood up and shook themselves off.

The *Kitty Clyde's Sister* and the *No Name* quickly followed suit. All the boats were safe now, and the expedition had traversed its first major canyon. Bradley compared the experience to that of

breaking a wild stallion. But there was one significant difference—
on the river you could drown.

On shore for the evening, the group spread their wet clothes
and blankets across the rocks to dry. They then went to work on
their usual duties. The Major and Bradley headed off on a geology hike, and Oramel Howland and Goodman climbed up a side
canyon to continue with mapmaking. Dunn was having trouble
with the barometers, so he remained in camp to tinker with the
infernal mercury tubes.

The hunters, who found the desert a greater challenge than
they expected, had no choice but to scour the banks for something
to eat. They killed several geese and a beaver, but the beaver sank
before they could get to it.

The next morning brought an early departure. Within minutes of shoving off, Bradley and Walter Powell got the *Maid of
the Canyon* hopelessly stuck on a sandbar, and they had to push
her off. A few miles downstream, Hawkins and Hall pinned *Kitty
Clyde's Sister* so firmly against a rock that they had to pry her off
with an oar.

It was clear that the rowing techniques of the oarsmen had not
significantly improved. Several valuable oars were lost to the river
that day. The party paused for a brief lunch, and they spent the rest
of the afternoon negotiating a series of small but exciting rapids.

The scenery here was magnificent. Grottoes were carved out of
the red sandstone by thin brooks, and mosses and ferns filled the
crevices. A narrow ribbon of blue etched the sky above. Camp was
unfurled beneath a large cottonwood full of warblers and larks,
and the men stayed up late around the campfire, talking about the
day's events and the dangers that lurked beyond.

The next day, the expedition approached a canyon whose walls
glowed a surreal shade of rose in the morning light. Large rocks

had fallen and were swept into the river by tributaries, and the boats were pushed along briskly by the feisty current. The explorers could tell that trouble lay ahead, and they landed above the rapids. A long, rocky ledge afforded a viewpoint of the river below, and they scurried up to see what loomed.

The men, full of anticipation, scanned the scene—a furious maelstrom of water pounding violently against rock. They stared into the chaos, searching for a clue to a route that might offer them safe passage through the mayhem beyond.

Mesmerized by this powerful force of nature, the men could not take their eyes off the recirculating maze of rock and suction holes. It was quickly apparent that it would be ludicrous to even consider entering the rapids.

Sumner and Dunn tossed several pieces of driftwood into the river to judge the speed and direction of the current. The results confirmed their suspicions. The driftwood floated along nicely until it encountered a reversal on the backside of a boulder, upended itself several times, disappeared, and then reappeared 20 yards downstream. The same fate obviously awaited the boats.

Bradley warned Sumner and Dunn that it simply could not be done. The Major studied the currents for another hour, then abruptly instructed the men to get ready for the descent.

The men looked at each other without saying a word. On the way to the boats, they stopped to urinate and relieve their stress. Out of earshot of Powell, they posed the question: If the Major is so confident the rapid can be run, why doesn't he row it himself?

The boats entered the current, and Powell directed Sumner and Dunn on the route to take through the rocky shoals that littered it. Within 30 seconds the run was over, and the *Emma Dean* wallowed out of control in the churning eddy below.

The other boats followed. Astonished with their success,

the men jumped up in the sloshing boats, slapping each other on their backs and laughing with joy at their unbelievably good fortune.

Immediately afterward, the canyon receded, and the sweeping valley known as Brown's Hole (now called Brown's Park) opened up. The area was designated as a "hole" because the early trappers chose a sheltered spot such as this in which to "hole up" during stormy weather. The exhausted crew pleaded with the Major to spend a few days in this paradise, and so they did. On June 2, Sumner wrote of the delightful valley:

> *Spread our blankets on the clear, green grass, with no roof but the old pines above us, through which we could see the sentinel stars shining from the deep blue pure sky, like happy spirits looking through the blue eyes of a pure hearted woman.*

The river meandered among the steep and rugged mountains and plateaus for some 35 miles through a 5-mile-wide valley punctuated with meadows of tall grasses and groves of leafy cottonwoods and willow trees. The marshes were full of waterfowl, but the hunters had little luck in securing dinner. Seneca Howland shot a rattlesnake, but unfortunately that was the extent of his contribution to the community larder.

At the end of Brown's Hole, the Green River soon left Utah and entered Colorado. Major Powell wrote on June 3:

> *The little valleys above are beautiful peaks; between the peaks are stately pine forests, half hiding ledges of red sandstone. Mule deer and elk abound; grizzly bears, too, are abundant; wild cats, wolverines, and mountain lions are here at home. The forest aisles are filled with the music of birds, and the peaks*

are decked with flowers. Noisy brooks meander through them; ledges of moss-covered rock are seen; and gleaming in the distance are the snowfields, and the mountain tops are away in the clouds.

The men were relieved to be alive, and the joy of reveling in this simple fact was evident in camp that night.

CHAPTER NINE

THE PLEASANT LIFE OF THE PAST SEVERAL DAYS changed dramatically with the expedition's entrance to a spectacular 2,000-foot gash in the Precambrian rock. Powell described it simply as "a black portal to a region of gloom."

Due to its north-south orientation, the precipitous and barren canyon was almost always shrouded in dark shadow. Two weeks into the journey, the men were only 150 miles from where they started.

Amid the incessant, reverberating roar of whitewater slamming against red and purple rock, the men continued downstream with railway speed. The canyon was named Lodore at the suggestion of Andy Hall, the young Scot, who was reminded of a few lines of a poem by Robert Southey that he memorized in childhood:

> *Advancing and prancing and glancing and dancing,*
> *recoiling, turmoiling and toiling and boiling, . . .*
> *And so never ending, but always descending,*
> *sounds and motions for ever and ever are blending,*
> *all at once and all over, with a mighty uproar,*
> *and this way the water comes down at Lodore.*

Not everyone in the group approved. Sumner for one objected; diving into the "musty trash" of Europe to find names for new discoveries was, to his mind, distinctly un-American.

The next week—and 20 miles of river—was disastrous. The current that swept into the walls of the canyon—which in many places rose straight up from the water's edge—typically began with strong, sleek tongues thrusting into massive boulders. Stair-step drops complicated the passage through this narrow course of naked splendor. The maelstrom then ended in massively large tail waves capable of devouring a boat.

The shale canyon overhead often turned to a variety of crags, ribbed walls, pinnacled crests, amphitheaters, and alcoves of astounding beauty and grandeur. It was Sunday, and Bradley said he was offended that the Major failed to observe the Sabbath. In Bradley's view, supernatural forces were involved in the majesty before them:

> *The scenery is at this point sublime. The red sand-stone rises on either side more than 2,000 feet, shutting out the sun for much of the day while at our feet the river, lashed to a foam, rushes on with indescribable fury. O how great is He who holds in the hollow of his hand what pygmies we who strive against it.*

On June 7, Major Powell too remarked on the overwhelming beauty of the place:

> *This evening, as I write, the sun is going down, and the shadows are settling in the canyon. The vermillion gleams and roseate hues, blending with the green and gray tints, are slowly changing to somber brown above, and black shadows are creeping over them below; and now it is a dark portal to a region*

*of gloom—the gateway through which we are to enter on our
voyage of exploration tomorrow. What shall we find?*

The next day—barely two weeks into the journey and five
miles into Lodore Canyon—the men in the *Emma Dean* heard
the familiar sound of rapids ahead. The deep roar ricocheted off
the canyon walls, and sunshine only briefly penetrated the gloomy
depths. Shafts of filtered light played ominously on the jagged
boulders that littered the riverbed, and the river reflected fiery hues
of quartzite above. Marbled with silt, the river—a rich, milky tan
purling downstream—made a dramatic turn and then disappeared
out of sight.

The Major ordered Sumner and Dunn to land the boat, and he
signaled the other boats to do the same. The *Maid of the Canyon*
and *Kitty Clyde's Sister* followed closely behind. Satisfied with
their course, Powell jumped to shore and began walking downriver, hopping from boulder to boulder to scout rapids that dropped
some 35 feet in half a mile.

At the last moment, Powell looked up and saw the *No Name*,
with the Howland brothers and Goodman on board, in the middle
of the river. The men were oblivious to Powell and the hazards that
lay ahead. Powell screamed and waved, but to no avail.

The crew of the *No Name*, busy with bailing out water from the
previous rapids, may have missed the Major's signal. Or it may have
been the Major's fault. Sumner wrote:

*As Major Powell was the only free-handed man [the only one
not rowing] in the outfit, he was supposed always to attend to it
[signaling the other boats where to go in the rapids], but I fear
he got too badly rattled to attend to it properly on several occasions, notably so at Disaster Falls in Lodore Canyon.*

Some have even speculated that the crew of the *No Name* may have been drinking. In any event, it was too late to avoid the catastrophe that was about to befall them.

After stalling momentarily in the slack water at the head of the rapids, the *No Name* was swept into the powerful jaws of the rapid. Powell ran after the boat as it careened downstream and out of control. The Major knew full well the fatal consequences of losing a boat, along with a third of the expedition's food and supplies.

By this time, the Howland brothers were rowing furiously to move the boat to the bank. The boat fell into the first drop and stalled briefly. The second waterfall, which was far worse, lay just beyond, and the drop was an abrupt 20 feet.

The *No Name* somehow managed to survive both falls.

The boat was rapidly gaining speed when it struck a huge red rock that sat midstream. The impact of the boat against the boulder propelled the three men into the river. The boat jammed briefly against another rock, which allowed time for the men to grab the gunwales of the boat and pull themselves inside.

Full of water, and now weighing 7,000 or 8,000 pounds, the craft was unmanageable as it wallowed down the cataract and into the bouncing tail waves.

The real problems then began. Several hundred yards downstream was a set of rapids more ferocious than the first. The facial expressions of the men revealed that they recognized their impending fate. There was nothing they could do but hold on.

The quickly moving boat drifted toward the center of the river, where it struck a huge boulder broadside with a terrific force. Quivering briefly, the *No Name* boat snapped in half like a dry tree limb. The crack reverberated off the canyon walls like a rifle shot.

The men vanished immediately into the river's foam.

Powell continued to chase after the boat, and the others followed after him. Rounding a bend in the river, they spotted the Howland brothers and Goodman on a small island in the middle of the current. Goodman was desperately clinging to a rock, and Oramel was trying to reach him from the shore. Seneca had just crawled out of the river.

The dilemma now was how to get the three men out of the center of the river and back to shore. Sumner suggested to Powell that he row the *Emma Dean* alone to attempt a rescue. Powell was reluctant to place another boat—and his head boatman—at risk, but there was no other choice.

Sumner untied the boat, pushed off, and aimed the bow toward the island where the three men were stranded. As he sped downstream, he narrowly missed the powerful hydraulics that finished off the *No Name*. He positioned the bow close enough that the men could jump in before the current swept them downstream. Heaving on the oars, Sumner was just able to reach the bank before the next set of drops.

With that drama behind them, the expedition's attention was now focused on what was left of the *No Name*. The boat appeared to be lost forever, along with its contents—a third of the party's food, all the clothing of the Howlands and Goodman, a number of important maps and topographical notes, and most important, the barometers.

No one could explain why all the barometers had been placed in one boat, rather than distributed among them, but it was an error of tragic proportions. The loss of the instruments would not only compromise the scientific mission but also increase the danger of getting lost since the expedition could not be sure of its elevation. Calculation of the expedition's location depended almost entirely upon the lost barometers.

The Major ran up and wildly poked his finger into Oramel Howland's chest. Furious, the Major screamed at the top of his lungs for an explanation. A fire came into his eyes that none of the men had seen before. Howland, dripping wet, dropped his head, shook it, and slowly walked away.

Powell described the scene a little differently in his report: "We were as glad to shake hands with them as though we had been on voyage around the world and wrecked on a distant coast."

The recollections of the other members made clear that the incident was the beginning of a troubled relationship between the Major and the Howland brothers and Dunn that grew increasingly bitter as the expedition progressed downstream.

That night in camp the men spoke very little to one another. The Major took his dinner alone, and he was seething with anger. He told his brother Walter that the incident upstream constituted gross negligence. As he spoke, he turned increasingly bitter toward the men involved.

The loss of the *No Name* and all its supplies was bad enough. The ten men would of course have to be redistributed among the remaining three boats. The maps and notes that had been washed overboard could not possibly be reconstructed.

Powell now faced the critical dilemma of whether to temporarily halt the expedition and walk out of the canyon to Salt Lake City, where barometers could be ordered from New York. That diversion would cost them valuable time, but more significantly, it would embarrass Powell for the ineptitude of his leadership.

After all, it was only day 16 of the journey. The expedition had averaged less than ten miles of progress a day.

Bradley summed up the situation regarding the loss of the *No Name* in his journal: "It is a serious loss to us and we are rather low spirited. Tonight we must camp right at the head of a roaring rapid more than a mile in length and in which we have already lost one of our boats and nearly lost three of our number."

The next morning, the bright orange sun crept over the lip of the canyon walls, and the men saw that the *No Name* had washed farther downstream. The boat lay exposed on a sandbar closer to shore, and her broken stern was just slightly visible. Sumner and Hall volunteered to swim to the craft and collect whatever gear they could. Seeing no other alternative, Powell agreed.

The two men managed to reach the wreck, pull themselves inside, and rummage through the contents. Surprisingly enough, there, among the soggy contents, were the barometers, which Sumner and Hall waved proudly in the air. When the package was brought to shore, they discovered—even more miraculously—that the instruments were intact.

From the boat's bow, Hall also retrieved a ten-gallon keg of whiskey that had been secretly stashed there. Even though alcohol was prohibited, Powell was so ecstatic at the recovery of the barometers that he encouraged the men to have a round of drinks. During the ensuing revelry, the men decided there was only one appropriate name for the rapids: Disaster Falls.

Even amid their efforts to survive, the men had had time to enjoy the remarkable beauty and grandeur of the scenery surrounding them—the remarkable bluffs and cliffs, peaks and crags, and amphitheaters and alcoves.

After the accident at Disaster Falls, the party required regrouping. With one less boat, there was the issue of where to put the three men. It was decided to place Goodman in the *Emma Dean* with Major Powell, Sumner, and Dunn, making the small craft extremely overcrowded. Seneca Howland moved to *Maid of the Canyon* with Bradley and Walter Powell, and Oramel Howland inhabited *Kitty Clyde's Sister* with Hawkins and Hall.

Disaster Falls, as the party discovered, was in reality a series of six separate rapids that dropped 25 feet in the course of a mile—an extremely steep descent. And even more amazing, the party had only negotiated the first of the rapids.

Unfortunately, there was an even bigger problem ahead. The stair-step falls occurred within such quick succession that if one lost control of the boat for even a second, the consequences could be fatal. The bolder-embedded cataract embodied every obstacle possible in a rapid—wide chutes, 90-degree turns, constricted narrows, huge boulders, powerful eddies, deep holes, tail waves, swirling boils, and overhanging cliffs. The powerful current plowed itself into these whitewater hazards at a furious pace.

To mentally photograph each segment of the rapid—and its relationship to the sections above and below it—was virtually impossible. To piece it all together was especially difficult when a boater was in the middle of the river and moving along at breakneck speed. Matters were made worse by the variety of obstacles that were not visible from the shore.

A rower who veered sideways in the large waves at the head of the rapids found himself in a precarious situation. It was almost impossible to regain sufficient control to avoid the rock-infested maelstrom that signaled the lower falls.

In spite of the difficulties posed by the rapids, Bradley remained good-natured about the fate of the endeavor: "I fell today while trying to save my boat from a rock and have a bad cut over the left eye which I fear will make an ugly scar. But what odds, it can't disfigure my ugly mug and it may improve it, who knows?"

The lower falls, dropping a significant 15 feet in very short order, were perhaps worse than anything that lay upstream. The cataract swept underneath an overhanging ledge on river right, and it threatened to decapitate anything that came near it. The men had no other choice—they were forced to line the boats around the rapids, a back-breaking process of pushing and pulling the boats around boulders in the river and then hauling the gear along the banks to the quiet water below.

Struggling to control a bucking boat and gear weighing more than two tons with a rope from shore was only slightly less dangerous than running the rapids.

Even on shore, it seemed, the descent downriver was a perilous one indeed.

CHAPTER TEN

In Disaster Falls, the men miraculously survived what Sumner called "a hell of foam." It was a formidable stretch of whitewater—practically one continuous rapid that was almost 15 miles long and dropped some 300 feet.

The loss of the *No Name*, along with a third of the party's food, much of its valuable equipment, and the clothing for its three occupants, was catastrophic enough. But the more serious consequence was the declining morale of the expedition.

It was startlingly clear to the men that lives could have been lost in the mishap at Disaster Falls. The expedition was forced to take a more guarded approach to the rapids, a process that dramatically slowed the expedition's progress downstream and stretched their food supplies even farther.

Knowing that the accident at Disaster Falls could have been averted with the exercise of more caution did not make matters any easier. The incident was the start of the increasing tension that developed between the Major and his brother on one side and the Howland brothers and Bill Dunn on the other.

Below Disaster Falls, the river did not let up. The current continued its hard-charging pace through a winding canyon where close-set boulders blocked the flow in midchannel. These distinct waterfalls were made all the more challenging by the tight S-curves they formed. The current required not only precise maneuvering skills but good fortune to survive it.

After the expedition's experience at Disaster Falls, Powell concluded that it was foolish to even consider running the next set of rapids. None of the men disagreed.

Powell made the decision to have the crew portage the first two falls and line the third. Sumner suggested—perhaps only half jesting—that it might be better to simply shove the boats into the current and pick up whatever was left of them downstream.

Bradley wrote on June 11:

> *Have been working like galley-slaves all day. Have lowered the boats all the way with ropes and once unloaded and carried the goods around one very bad place. The rapid is still continuous and not improving. Where we are tonight roars and foams like a wild beast.*

It took a full day for the men to work their way around the rapids, and they spent a restless night on a rocky ledge with barely enough room to lie down. Bradley described the campsite selection: "The Major as usual has chosen the worst camping-ground possible. If I had a dog lie where my bed is made tonight I would kill him and burn his collar and swear I never owned him."

The next day the bigger issue was how to descend the churning water below. The river fell three stories in less than half a mile, and the rapid was full of currents containing complicated routes through a maze of house-sized boulders. The crux of the rapid was the mass of impenetrable red quartzite rocks that had fallen from the canyon walls to create this madness. These obstacles almost completely dammed the river, forming a phalanx to river right.

The only runnable channel seemed to be a narrow one on river left. It was a thin tongue that sent the current first into a huge boulder on one side, and then a hundred yards downstream into several large holes on the other. To avoid coming to terms with this imposing threat, it was necessary for the oarsmen to execute a very precise entry. This was not an easy task with boats loaded as heavily as theirs.

Past this sentinel rock, the river dropped through a complex series of rock gardens and chutes. A successful negotiation of the hazards demanded an uncommon degree of both finesse and luck. The chances of colliding broadside with a boulder or breaking an oar became a likely probability because of the skillful maneuvering required to dodge the quickly approaching hazards.

After losing the *No Name* in Disaster Falls, the party could ill afford to risk a capsize, so they walked around the rapids they called Hell's Half Mile. Portaging was their only option. The men began to move the mounds of boats and equipment alongside the shore to the bottom of the rapids. At this point, they certainly had "hell" to pay.

To add insult to injury, as the party unloaded the boats and Hawkins started a campfire to prepare dinner, a sudden gust of wind swept the embers into the dry grass and brush, and the entire shore suddenly burst into flames. The men ran for their lives to escape the fire, but the sheer cliffs prevented their escape, so they headed toward the boats and the river.

Oramel Howland recounted the harrowing incident:

> One of the crew came in hatless, another shirtless, a third without his pants, and a hole burned in the posterior portion of his

*drawers, another with nothing but drawers and shirt, and still
another had to pull off his handkerchief from his neck which
was all ablaze. With the loss of his eyelashes and brows, and
a favorite moustache, and scorching of his ears, no other harm
was done. One of the party had gathered up our mess kit and
started hastily for the boat, but the smoke and heat was so
blinding that in his attempt to spring from the shore to the boat
he lost his footing and fell, mess kit and all, in about ten feet
of water, that put him out (I mean the fire in his clothes) and
he crawled over the side of the boat as she was being pushed off,
not worse, but better, if possible, for his ducking. Our mess kit,
however was lost, as also a number of other things, of which we
felt the need quite often.*

Howland listed the contents of the mess kit, which consisted of
the following usual—and not-so-usual—items:

> *One gold pan, used for making bread*
> *One bake oven, with broken lid*
> *One camp kettle, for making tea or coffee*
> *One frying pan*
> *One large spoon and two tea spoons*
> *Three tin plates and five bailing cups*
> *One pickax and one shovel*

With a touch of humor, Howland described the party's use of
these kitchen utensils:

> *The last two articles we do not use on ordinary occasions, but
> when a pot of beans, which by the way is a luxury, is boiled in
> place of tea or coffee, our cook sometimes uses the latter article*

[the shovel] for a spoon, and the former [the pickax] to clean his teeth after our repast is over.

At long last, the expedition arrived at quiet waters. The river flattened out as it purled beneath a long, spectacular, and vertical corridor of reddish-yellow Weber Sandstone that was 600 to 800 feet high. The Yampa River, flowing through a corridor of gray sandstone, entered from the east among a thick growth of box elder and cottonwoods.

The silence of the place invited the men to call out, only to have their words returned to them from the massive cliff. The expedition named it Echo Park, now a part of Dinosaur National Park.

Already the resentments among the men—particularly those aimed toward the Major—were beginning to reveal themselves. Sumner complained:

All hands pulled with a will, except the Professor and Mr. Howland. The Professor being a one-armed man, he was set to watching the geese, while Howland was perched on a sack of flour in the middle of one of the large boats, mapping the river as we rowed along.

Next came Whirlpool Canyon, whose eroded strata descended in sweeping curves of pink and purple, along with sharp pinnacles, thin-crusted ridges, and tall crags that had resisted the erosion. Evergreen trees, offering a pleasant contrast to the bare rock, were abundant. Around the protruding buttresses and into the recesses of the canyon, the river rolled, boiled, and churned, and the spinning current was sent into powerful whirlpools.

On June 22, about a month after the expedition began, the river emerged from the upturned sedimentary formations of Whirlpool Canyon near the boundary of Colorado. This was a beautiful valley, full of verdant meadows, called Island Park. Here the swirling waters of the Green River entered Utah in a brilliant red sandstone chasm called Split Mountain Canyon, full of crags, pinnacles, and natural monuments.

The river then broadened and meandered its way through vegetated bottomlands and sandy islands on its tortured path downstream toward hazards the expedition could not fathom.

PART III

DESOLATION, GRAY, AND LABYRINTH CANYONS

DAYS 34–55:
JUNE 26–JULY 17

★ ★ ★ ★

BRIEF TIMELINE

June 28: Uinta River
July 9: Desolation Canyon
July 13: Gray Canyon
July 15: Labyrinth Canyon

CHAPTER ELEVEN

AFTER MIRACULOUSLY SURVIVING THE RIGORS offered up by cataracts inside the canyons of Lodore, Whirlpool, and Split Mountain, the expedition entered the wide expanse of the Uinta Valley. That valley extended for almost a hundred miles through low, rounded bluffs and rolling plains.

On June 26—the 34th day of the journey—Sumner expressed the expedition's relief at having left the canyons behind: "It was a welcome sight to us after two weeks of the hardest kind of work, in a canyon where we could not see half a mile, very often, in any direction except straight up."

The sky opened up, and the group's optimism improved along with it. The Uinta Valley was the longest break in the string of canyons that extends the length of the Green and Colorado Rivers. It offered a rest for the expedition after weeks of backbreaking toil in claustrophobic conditions that had severely tested the men's resolve.

The crew quickly took advantage of the slower pace offered by the quiet waters of the broad valley, and they relaxed in this bucolic stretch of river, where herds of antelope grazed in grassy meadows. Here the party found plenty of geese to shoot for dinner, and one afternoon they bagged ten of them, although the men commented that the birds were very poor eating. Near the river were remnants of tepee poles and campfires, clear signs that Indians had lived here in the past.

The party put in a respectable 23 miles on the first day out, and they spent the night on the east side of the river beneath three large cottonwoods. Sumner remarked:

> *Rested, eat [sic] supper, and turned in to be serenaded by the wolves, which kept up their howling until we dropped asleep, and I don't know how much longer, as I heard them the next morning at daybreak.*

The next day was another long one, and the party traveled a remarkable distance—63 miles, made possible by a current flowing at a brisk eight miles an hour—as they made up mileage in order to stay on schedule.

The men were impressed by the tremendous splendor of the valley, especially the sweeping curves of barren sandstone and shale that contrasted sharply with verdant islands in the middle of the river. Sumner pointed out that the splendid view changed with "kaleidoscopic rapidity." The hunters were able to kill eight more geese for dinner, and camp was made on the west bank near a thin, muddy creek.

All was well with the venture until a substantial nuisance arose (one that modern-day boaters can readily attest to): *hordes* of hungry mosquitoes. The men soon discovered that the little monsters were impossible to escape, and their incessant noise and painful bites drove them to distraction. Bradley commented:

> *As the mosquitoes drove me away before, I thought I would get ahead of them this time so I put a piece of mosquito bar over my*

*hand and fastened it around my waist and with gloves to pro-
tect my hands and a pair of boots coming to the knee to protect
me from rattlesnakes, I set out and after hunting along the side
of the Uinta River for more than a mile I succeeded in finding
just one bush which I broke down and brought off in triumph.
The mosquitoes are perfectly frightful. As I went through the
rank grass and wild sunflower sometimes higher than my head
they would fairly scream around me. I think I never saw them
thicker even in Florida than in this place.*

The only relief from the pests seemed to be a smoky campfire
to propel them away. Somehow Bradley managed to maintain his
sense of humor: "One of the men says that while out on the shore
of the lake a mosquito asked him for his pipe, knife and tobacco
and told him to hunt his old clothes for a match while he loaded
the pipe."

The next day was another exhausting one (48 miles in all), and
that afternoon, two days after leaving Split Mountain, the expedition arrived at the mouth of the Uinta River (now called the
Duchesne River). It was a major tributary flowing in from the west
through a corridor called Antelope Valley.

As usual, the group found a large cottonwood tree to camp
beneath, and there were, as always, mosquitoes: "The musical
little mosquitoes bite so badly that I can write no longer," Bradley
recorded in his diary.

The Uinta River was one of the few identifiable landmarks of
the expedition, as it was the former crossing of the Denver City
and Salt Lake City wagon road, established four years earlier. At
this spot, the U.S. Cavalry brought a train of 70 wagons, built a
ferry, crossed over, and then promptly sank the ferry boat.

Powell estimated the expedition had traveled roughly 350 miles from Green River Station. They had another 300 miles to go before arriving at the confluence of the Grand River.

Here, at the mouth of the Uinta, the party spent a week exploring the surrounding countryside of rich, tall grasses, taking longitude and latitude calculations of the nearby White River (another prominent landmark), and then walking to the agency for the Indian reservation some 40 miles away. The men seemingly had no fear of the Indians, and they built a large campfire to attract the attention of any natives in the neighborhood. None of them responded, to the disappointment of Bradley, at least.

The men were able to send and receive letters at the agency, and they busily wrote letters back home, many of which were promptly published in the local newspapers, turning the members of the expedition into something of national heroes. The area around the reservation, established in a treaty the previous year, was more populated than any they had traveled through, but the nearest signs of civilization were still days away.

The next morning Walter Powell and Andy Hall set out on the grueling walk to the agency, which required trudging through deep sands and then wading in the muddy river. Two days later, the men were joined by the Major and Goodman. The reservation was located in a splendid valley of pine groves, meadows, and clear streams. Powell took the opportunity to replenish some supplies, mostly flour, although the amount of provisions available was limited.

Powell also took advantage of the opportunity to visit the chief, Tsau-wi-at, said to be more than 100 years old, wizened and shrunken. In spite of the language barrier, Powell attempted to talk to him, and he offered several smoking pipes, which the chief gladly accepted.

The chief's influential wife, who was called "The Bishop" because of her important position on the council, was considerably younger and more coherent. She told Powell about her interest in developing modern agricultural methods for the tribe's impressive range of crops (wheat, potatoes, turnips, pumpkins, melons, and other vegetables).

For the most part, the members of the tribe still lived in tents, and they refused to build houses. When dwellings were previously built, they were, for superstitious reasons, burned to the ground when the occupant died. Powell spotted a number of ancient Indian ruins, but the locals claimed to know nothing about them. Over the next several days, Powell studied the language of the tribe and collected the articles they made.

Goodman, the tender-footed Englishman, decided he had had enough and left the expedition here. This was fortuitous, because the boats were heavily loaded and Goodman had contributed little to the venture. His departure freed up much-needed space in the Howlands' boat. Powell wrote:

Frank Goodman informs me, this morning, that he has concluded not to go on with the party, saying that he has seen danger enough. It will be remembered that he was one of the crew of the "No Name," when she was wrecked. As our boats are rather heavily loaded, I am content that he should leave, although he has been a faithful man.

Sumner had a similar reaction to the news of Goodman's departure:

Goodman, having had all the experience his health called for, stopped at the post. He had several close calls, and possibly ran out of nerve. He was a fine singer of sea songs, and we missed him around the evening camp.

While Powell and the others visited the reservation, the rest of the group remained in camp and amused themselves in a variety of ways: shooting geese and ducks on a nearby lake, picking currants, patching the boats, cleaning rusty rifles and pistols, and braving the mosquitoes.

The Fourth of July arrived. In a gesture of patriotism, the men unfurled the flag. Memories of home and previous celebrations filled their minds. Bradley, the most sentimental among them, wrote:

> *Took a long walk tonight alone beside the lake and thought of home, contrasted its comforts and privileges with the privations we suffer here and asked myself why am I here? But those green flowery graves on the hillside far away seem to answer for me, and with moistened eyes I seek again my tent where engaged with my own thought, I pass hours with my friend at home, sometimes laughing, sometimes weeping until sleep comes and dreams bring me into the apparent presence of those I love.*

The next day the Powells and Hall returned to the river on horseback with several Ute guides and two pack animals loaded with 300 pounds of flour and various kitchen utensils. Not everyone was pleased with the amount of food the Major returned with, but Powell quickly dismissed the criticism. Sumner complained:

> *Major Powell was gone five days and brought back a shirttail of supplies. I thought at the time it was a damned stingy, foolish scheme, as there was plenty of supplies to be had, to bring back such a meager mess for nine to make a thousand-mile voyage through an unknown canyon, but as I wasn't boss I suppose I ought to keep still about it.*

The expedition was far behind schedule. They were only 43 days away from the put-in, and they had progressed only about 200 miles—with almost 800 more to go. At this rate the expedition would most certainly never complete its mission.

On July 6 the party arrived a few miles downstream at the White River entering from the east. They spotted a nearby island containing a small crop of potatoes, beets, carrots, and turnips. No one was tending the farm and none of the crops were ripe, but Hall suggested that the tops of the vegetables would make good "greens." Hawkins cooked them for lunch.

An hour later the men became violently ill and vomited everything they had consumed. Powell wrote that the men "tumble around under the trees, groaning with pain, and I feel a little alarmed, lest our poisoning be severe." Sumner described the incident in his typical lighthearted way:

We pulled out and went down the river about ten miles to Johnston's Island, where a squaw man had planted a garden. Having landed, Hawkins and Hall started to investigate, and as they could not find anything else, they proposed to have a mess of greens. They proceeded to filch turnip tops, beet tops, potato tops, and God knows what else. They brought a backload of the beastly stuff, dumped it into the boats, and we ran down the river a few miles and landed again for dinner. Hawkins cooked a kettle of his plunder, poured it into the gold pan and yelled, "Grub pile."

We proceeded to devour it to show our appreciation of his ability as a first-class cook. We had not gone a mile after dinner until all hands, the cook included, wished Johnston and his garden in the middle kettle of the lower world. Such a gang of sick men I never saw before or since. Whew! It seems I can feel it yet. I remarked to Hall that I didn't think potato tops made a good greens for the sixth day of July. He ripped out an oath or two, and swore he had coughed up a potato vine a foot long, with a potato on it as big as a goose egg.

Fortunately, the episode was brief, and they were able to resume by the middle of the afternoon.

Whitewater rapids, the party discovered, are not the only hazard encountered on an exploration of this magnitude.

CHAPTER TWELVE

LEAVING THE PLEASANT PACE OF THE UINTA VALLEY behind them, Powell and his crew entered a barren badlands dotted with a fascinating array of pinnacles and buttes. To add to the desolation, the temperature soared and the hot winds blew, further sapping the strength of the men.

On July 7, the wide valley quickly came to an end, and it was replaced by a canyon of striking yellow-colored sandstones. The expedition soon encountered some of the Green River's finest sculpted chasms, aptly named Desolation and Gray Canyons.

Here the flow of the river spilled into towering gray, tan, and brown cliffs, often beautifully terraced, while light danced wildly on its swirling surface. The men frequently climbed to the rim thousands of feet above the river to survey the arid and deeply incised terrain that stretched before them like a lunar landscape.

Throughout the length of Desolation Canyon the descent of the Green was dramatic and the rapids were numerous. High terraced walls rose overhead, and their faces were carved with various buttes and castellated forms that had been eroded over the ages.

The fascinating array of crags, pinnacles, and tower-shaped peaks sped by as the party quickly moved downriver.

The strata among the walls were shades of yellow, gray, green, black, and red, and the colors were often blended together. There was little vegetation, and the monotony was broken only by an occasional thorny bush rooted in a handful of soil.

The canyon, featuring walls more than 1,500 feet high, started to close in, and with that came the rapids. Several good runs were made throughout the day, and 40 miles of river were promptly put behind the expedition. The men killed two otter and four geese, and they made camp on the east bank among a few small cedars.

In his usual poetic manner, the Major described the beauty they beheld before them:

> *We find quiet water today, the river sweeping in great and beautiful curves, the canyon walls steadily increasing in altitude. The escarpment formed by the cut edges of the rock are often vertical, sometimes terraced, and in some places the tread of the terraces are sloping. In these quiet curves vast amphitheaters are formed, now in vertical rocks, now in steps.*

Consistent with his tradition of naming topographical formations after members of the expedition, Powell decided to designate a graceful and symmetrical formation as Sumner's Amphitheater.

On July 8, three of the men—the Major, Walter, and Bradley—climbed to the top of the cliffs, a strenuous proposition in this terrain. Bradley noted that the scenery from the top was "wild and desolate," and that a "succession of craggy peaks like the one we were on was all we could see near us."

On the top, an interesting problem arose: The Major, with most of his right arm missing, could not pull himself up the cliff. Bradley was positioned above him, but did not have a rope. A simple but unique solution presented itself: Bradley took off his pants and dangled them in front of the Major, who reached out to grab them and pull himself up.

For the next three days, the river coursed through the canyon in a long, wide meander, but it gradually picked up speed and became more and more unpredictable, requiring the expedition to frequently line the boats.

Bradley wrote:

Since we started today we have had a succession of bad rapids, but have run them all, though one I think was the worst we had ever run. Every boat was half full of water when we got through. It is a wild exciting game, and aside from the danger of losing our provisions and having to walk out to civilization I should like to run them all for the danger to life is only trifling.

Camp that evening was pitched on the east side of the river among clumps of sage and greasewood. The men were tired, wet, and hungry. Soon the bread was baking in the Dutch oven, the coffee pot was steaming away, and the smell of bacon permeated the air. The sound of rushing river was the first and last thing the men heard that day.

The next day began with winds sweeping through Desolation Canyon, described by Bradley:

A terrible gale of dry hot wind swept through our camp and roared through the canyon mingling its sound with the hollow roar of the cataract making music fit for the infernal regions. We needed only a few flashes of lightning to meet Milton's most vivid conceptions of Hell. The sand from the beach buried our beds while that from an island below filled the air until the canyon was no comfortable place of repose as one had to cover his head to get his breath.

The river currents don't cooperate either. A constant stream of rapids more than 20 miles long kept the men on edge, with hardly time to empty the boat before the next round of whitewater began. To make matters worse, the expedition's state of provisions was exceedingly low, and they were only six weeks into the journey.

The foam and fury became so severe in places that the party was forced to line the rapids. Losing a boat—and the resulting overland trek out of these 4,000-foot canyon walls—would most likely be fatal.

Bradley wrote about the expedition's routine in negotiating the rapids of Desolation Canyon:

A succession of rapids or rather a continuous rapid with a succession of cataracts for 20 miles kept our nerves drawn up to their greatest tension. We would dash through one with the speed of the wind, round two in the eddy and pull for shore sometimes with little water on board but frequently half full, bail out and having looked a moment to see the best channel through the next, repeat the same thing, dashing and dancing like so many furies. Twice we let down with ropes but we could have run them all if it had become a necessity to do so. We are quite careful now of our provisions as the hot blasts that sweep through these rocky gorges admonish us that a walk out to civilization is almost certain death, so better go a little slow and safe.

On July 10, the party remained in camp for the day. Sumner was tinkering with the sextant, and Powell, Dunn, and Howland made their way to the top of the cliffs for altitude readings. The plateau on which they were standing was 8,000 feet above sea level, and they did not arrive back in camp until well after dark.

Bradley spent an interesting afternoon with Hall:

Andy is singing for his own amusement and my edification a song that will no doubt some day rank with America and other national anthems. All I can make out as he tears it out with a voice like a crosscut saw is the chorus: "When he put his arm around her she hustified like a forty pounder, look away, look away, look away in Dixie's land."

The precipices surrounding the expedition, barren and desolate as they were, reached magnificent proportions, with only the occasional cedar and greasewood to add color to the scene. As the expedition progressed downstream, the canyon grew more somber and mysterious as the sun began to set. The summits around them remained bright from the western rays long after the river itself had grown dim. A strange, enchanted light blended the transition from day to night.

The next day the expedition approached a rapid that seemed at first no more difficult than others they had encountered. The *Emma Dean* entered the fray, but the current strongly rushed into a rock wall, causing the rowers to lose an oar and break another.

The oarsmen tried to land the boat but were incapable of avoiding a massive wave that struck them with full force, turning the boat upside down and pouring the men into the tumultuous waves.

Swimming for his life, Powell succeeded in reaching the boat, and there he found Sumner and Dunn clinging desperately to its sides. With only one arm, Powell was unable to hang on for long, and when he let go he floated downstream with the aid of his life jacket. When the three of them reached the quiet water below the rapids, Sumner and Dunn righted the craft and were able to pull the Major inside.

In his diary, Powell made the boast that in the turbulent water he found "swimming is very easy" and that "he cannot sink." What he failed to mention was that he was wearing a life preserver, unlike Sumner and Dunn.

The losses that the *Emma Dean* sustained in the upset were significant: $800 worth of watches, $300 in cash belonging to the Major, two valuable guns, a barometer, and a roll of blankets. Sumner quipped, "I lost my temper and at least a year's growth—didn't have anything else to lose."

Building a large fire on the shore, the men dried their clothing. They fashioned much-needed oars out of driftwood. The total distance for the day—a dismal half a mile. Dinner was a couple of otters that came too close to Sumner's pistol, but he remarked that they were inedible.

The next day the expedition ran several more rapids—long, narrow chutes free of rocks. But nothing lasts forever, and soon the walls became precipitous again. Combined with disorderly piles of boulders and swirling waves, they created formidable whitewater hazards ahead.

In the one rapid that Bradley referred to as "an old roarer," the *Maid of the Canyon* was completely swamped. Bradley was knocked overboard, and after his foot was caught under the seat, he was dragged head down until the worst of the rapids was passed. He was finally hauled in.

Bradley recounted that he "got the boat on shore without any loss or inconvenience except a glorious ducking and a slight cut of one of my legs which I got when I was knocked overboard."

It was another long day, and in the process the men ran ten rapids and portaged 20 more, including a tricky one that pulsed beneath an overhanging cliff. The total run for the day was a very respectable 16 miles.

Camp that evening was made on a long and narrow sandbar. The hard work of the day—lowering the boats by lines, wading alongside them to push them farther into the current, clinging to their sides when the bed of the river fell out from beneath them, and pulling them back into the shallows at the end of the rapids— caused the party to collapse from exhaustion.

Just below this point, the men emerged from the red canyon walls into low bluffs, leaving the 97 miles of Desolation Canyon behind. It was July 13. The party put 18 miles—and 19 rapids—behind it that morning, then entered the gray sandstone of Coal Canyon (later renamed Gray Canyon).

In Gray Canyon there was a marked change in geology. The fossil-filled beds, long absent, appeared again. The canyon walls were buff in color, with seams of black coal and lignite appearing in places. The cliffs along the river were about 300 feet high, with jagged heights reaching almost 2,000 feet. Huge blocks of rock that had fallen into the river made for rough water that put the oarsmen on edge as they made their way downstream.

Hot winds continued throughout the day, and the current sped the expedition toward the confluence with the Grand River, where the two rivers become the Colorado. Bradley recorded his hope that "they may have an easier time in the Colorado," although he cautiously added: "We are prepared, however, to take it as it comes."

Another mile or so and the canyon walls rose again. A challenging set of rapids lay ahead, but there was no place to land the boats and lower them down, so the party was forced to balance themselves on slippery rocks in the channel of the river.

At this point, the walls of gray sandstone were a thousand feet high, and they enclosed the river for 60 miles. Fortunately, the current was benign, and the party moved downstream quickly as they rowed with all their might. The slower current offered a little breathing room for the explorers after the strenuous time in Desolation Canyon.

The 36 miles of Gray Canyon were soon passed before arriving at Gunnison Valley. The expedition had now descended a significant drop of 2,000 feet since starting the journey at Green River Station seven weeks earlier.

Below the massive sandstone tower known as Gunnison Butte, the party entered a truly desolate—and surreal—landscape. Powell described the terrain ahead:

> Extensive sand plains extend back from the immediate river valley, as far we can see, on either side. These naked, drifting sands gleam brilliantly in the midday sun of July. The reflected heat from the glaring surface produces a curious motion of the atmosphere; little currents are generated and the whole seems to be trembling and moving about in many directions, or, failing to see that the movement is in the atmosphere, it gives the impression of an unstable land. Plains, and hills, and cliffs, and distant mountains seems vaguely to be floating about in a trembling, wave-rocked sea, and patches of landscape will seem to float away, and be lost, and then reappear.

The party arrived at an Indian crossing, complete with crudely constructed log rafts, at the spot where Captain Gunnison of the

U.S. Army crossed the river while surveying for the railroad in 1853. Before leaving here, Gunnison established the latitude and longitude of the crossing that afterward bore his name. He was killed shortly thereafter by the Ute tribe.

Sixteen years later, the Powell expedition was well aware how fortunate they were to have traveled through these lonely and rugged chasms with no human casualties.

CHAPTER THIRTEEN

As the expedition left Gunnison Crossing, the Green River appeared to be in no hurry to make its way to the confluence of the Grand River, where the waters of the two rivers quietly merge to form the Colorado.

In between the party's present positon and the unison of the rivers downstream were two relatively short but undeniably spectacular chasms. They were aptly named Labyrinth and Stillwater Canyons. The men found the majesty of their lonely depths to be quite stirring, and the entries in their diaries reflected their astonishment at the natural beauty they found there.

The current below Gunnison Crossing was placid, and on July 14 Bradley recorded his thoughts about the vastness of the landscape that surrounded them:

> *The whole country is inconceivably desolate, as we float along on a muddy stream walled in by huge sand-stone bluffs that echo back the slightest sound. Hardly a bird save the ill-omened raven or an occasional eagle screaming over us; one feels a sense of loneliness as he looks on the little party, only three boats and*

nine men, hundreds of miles from civilization, bound on an errand the issue of which everybody declares must be disastrous. Yet if he could enter our camp at night or our boats by day he could read the cool deliberate determination to persevere that possesses every man of the party and would at once predict that the issue of all would be success.

The expedition at this point was still almost 600 miles away from the end of their journey. They floated through a wide valley lined with stone walls and hardly a plant to break the barrenness. Toward the east could be seen the Sierra La Sal, two clusters of rounded peaks some 50 miles away and truly majestic in their alpine splendor. The occasional small cottonwood along the river suggested the group's campsite each evening.

The river soon left the shale formations and entered layers of gray and pink sandstone. The buttes along the banks often turned to monoliths several hundred feet high, and many of these looked like castles, complete with turrets and battlements. The river took endless turns through these still waters, and the surreal colors of the canyon were mysteriously muted by the masses of clouds floating overhead.

Along its path downriver, the expedition stopped at the San Rafael River, a robust tributary entering from the west. Here the men found numerous arrowheads and well-worn Indian trails worthy of further investigation.

At this point Sumner made a curious comment about the morale of the expedition less than two months after its departure:

Another chapter of the Powell–Howland squabble was commenced as we left the camp near the San Rafael—a sad, bitter business. I wish I had put a stop to it long before I did. Things might have ended differently.

Sumner was no doubt referring to the unfortunate loss of the *No Name* at Disaster Falls in Lodore Canyon, which eventually led to the departure of the Howland brothers and Bill Dunn in the waning days of the journey.

The precipitous orange walls of Labyrinth Canyon consisted largely of sandstone, intricately and marvelously carved by the wind and water over the eons into a million different shapes. During rainstorms, sheets of water poured over the cliffs in muddy torrents of various hues of the earth. These waterfalls plunged hundreds of feet and then vanished into spray as the exquisite forces of nature they are. When the rain stopped, the wet brown sandstone contrasted sharply with the dark gray sky above.

The boaters floated on a serene current meandering through a vast assortment of rock formations high above—buttes, pinnacles, turrets, spires, castles, gulches, and alcoves of all kinds. These perpendicular cliffs of Navajo sandstone—with their red, amber, and chocolate layers—were curiously stained with jet-black sheets and streamers of desert varnish.

Small side canyons entered so closely together they sometimes appeared to be single alcoves—each full of glens, small canyons, and gorges with overhanging walls, amphitheaters, and overhanging shelves. The expedition felt as if it had entered a strange and forbidden realm.

The brilliant rays of sunshine appeared. The men hiked to the edge of the canyon's rim. Viewed from the top, the buttes, ridges, and mountains they beheld almost blended together, and the river was so lost in the layers that its existence a mile away would never be suspected. At night the men huddled around the campfire, and the pots of supper were soon boiling.

The days were fiery hot, as the men bent and pulled on the oars to inch their way down the river. Bradley wrote, "The sun was so hot we could scarcely endure it and much of the time the canyon was so closely walled in that the breeze could not reach us."

The overhanging cliffs, some reaching 600 feet high, were impressive in every sense of the word. They were often topped with vast barren domes and tall pinnacles and decorated with huge blind arches.

In spite of the majestic natural splendor surrounding them, the expedition continued to struggle. Bradley described the many difficulties they faced:

> *We have worked as hard as we could to get only 25 miles and the river has been so crooked that in going 20 miles we have actually advanced less than 11 miles. We have almost lost our trees. We stopped for dinner today in the open sun with the thermometer over one hundred degrees close to the water.*

Evidence of the ancient people—the Anasazi—who once lived here was ubiquitous. Ruins of the dwellings they built with large slabs of stone were explored by the Powell party, as well as the storage areas, petrified corncobs, earthen jars, basketry, and arrowheads that littered the terraces above the river.

After supper each night the men collected driftwood and built large campfires, gathered around them, and stared into the dark-blue heavens pin-pricked with bright constellations.

The expedition reached a great horseshoe bend in the river, veering first to the right for five miles, and then back to a point within a quarter of a mile from where it started. Another bend to the left extended nine miles and returned to itself within 600 yards. These two circuits suggested the name the men gave it: Bow-Knot Bend.

Powell, as usual, put his pen to good use in describing the scene before them:

There is an exquisite charm in our ride today down this beautiful canyon. It gradually grows deeper with every mile of travel; the walls are symmetrically curved, and grandly arched; of a beautiful color, and reflected in the quiet waters in many places, so as to almost deceive the eye, and suggest the thought to the beholder, that he is looking into profound departments. We are all in fine spirits, feel very gay, and the badinage of the men is echoed from wall to wall. Now and then we whistle, or shout, or discharge a pistol, to listen to the reverberation among the cliffs.

The 40 miles of Labyrinth Canyon was soon completed. The next day the expedition entered the 60 miles of Stillwater Canyon, and there was little change in the walls they found in Labyrinth. The buff sandstone was often mixed among red and orange sandstones, and the buttes were scattered among a surreal landscape of cones, buttresses, columns, and fantastically carved walls, some with deep alcoves and sudden recesses.

Powell spoke of the region as "a whole land of naked rock with giant forms carved on it; cathedral-shaped buttes towering hundreds or thousands of feet; cliffs that cannot be scaled, and canyon walls that shrink the river into insignificance, with vast hollow domes, tall pinnacles, and shafts set on the verge overhead, and all highly colored—buff, gray, red, brown, and chocolate; never lichened; never moss-covered; but bare, and often polished."

Despite such idyllic scenery, the party's problems persisted. The possibility of starving to death was real, and the men continued to grumble that Powell did not adequately reprovision the expedition with food at the agency for the reservation. Without medical supplies or training, even a simple illness or broken limb in these remote circumstances could prove fatal.

Poorly waterproofed, the gear sloshed around the porous compartments of the boats, and the result was a constant wetting of its contents, rendering much of the food inedible. The men were forced to constantly pull the boats out of the water to repair and re-caulk them before moving on to another dark and lonely abyss.

The party of explorers soon left the picturesque chasm of Stillwater Canyon behind. Now they anticipated seeing the confluence of the Green and the Grand.

Unbeknownst to the Powell expedition, the idyllic waters of Labyrinth and Stillwater Canyons were the calm before the storm.

CHAPTER FOURTEEN

As the Colorado River Exploring Expedition approached the juncture of the Green and Grand Rivers, they were well aware of those who had come before them.

The arrival of trappers in 1825 marked the first serious effort to explore these canyons. General William H. Ashley was the most distinguished among them. With six other men, Ashley constructed two makeshift boats of buffalo hides and descended the Green through its hazardous upper canyons—Flaming Gorge, Red, Lodore, Whirlpool, and Split Mountain. This was truly an impressive feat considering the problems that the Powell expedition encountered in the rapids of these chasms. Ashley scrawled his name and the year 1825 in dark letters on a boulder to mark his presence there.

When he reached the mouth of the Uinta River, Ashley cached his cargo and descended the Green another 50 miles before abandoning the project, almost starving to death in the process. A few newspapers reported the journey, but Ashley's full report was not published until 1918—long after Powell had passed through these canyons.

The Green River above the Uinta was prolific fur country, and the word quickly spread to other mountain men. Hunters like Jim Bridger and Kit Carson roamed the region, and they occasionally peered into the canyons to catch a glimpse of the river.

Before Major Powell arrived on the scene, there were only three other astronomically fixed points on the river between the Union Pacific railway at Green River Station, Wyoming, and the end of Grand Canyon. These were the mouth of the Uinta River, the mouth of Henry's Fork, and the mouth of Diamond Creek. With the exception of trails at Gunnison Butte (near present-day Green River City, Utah) and the Crossing of the Fathers (near what is now Lake Powell), very little was known about the Green below its confluence with the Uinta.

In the upper stretches of the Green River, then, there was a general idea of the character of the terrain and a rough appreciation of its topography. But it was still largely unknown wilderness, especially the land contiguous to the river.

On the Colorado River, the region south of the San Rafael River (near present-day Green River, Utah) to the Paria River (near present-day Lees Ferry, Arizona), and west to the high plateaus that form the southern continuation of the Wasatch Range (an area of at least 10,000 square miles), was completely unknown.

From the Paria River on down to Grand Wash Cliffs, the region north of the Colorado River was hardly better understood, although there were a few Mormon settlements on the headwaters of the Virgin River, as well as the recent settlement of Kanab farther east.

On the south side of the Colorado River, Lieutenant Joseph Ives had explored the area to some extent, having reached the river at the mouth of Diamond Creek. But he never reached the Grand Canyon north of Havasu Creek.

A decade of reports about the severity of the canyon below the confluence of the Green and Grand Rivers dissuaded anyone from attempting that stretch of the river. But a courageous mountain man named Denis Julien did take his chances in the lower canyon. A number of inscriptions carved by Julien and dated 1836 can be found along the river in Stillwater and Cataract Canyons. It is believed that he eventually lost his life in a treacherous stretch of river here.

Perhaps the most interesting story to come out of these canyons was the purported journey of James White in 1867. White claimed to be the first to navigate the canyons and rapids of the Colorado River on a raft made of driftwood logs. This was almost two years before Powell pushed off from the shores of Green River, Wyoming.

Powell heard about the feat several months before his expedition and interviewed White. Powell quickly dismissed the tale, as have the vast majority of those familiar with the river. But there remained a persistent following who insisted that White had done what he claimed. These individuals were tenacious enough that they were able to convince Congress to recognize White for the first descent.

The unadorned story that White first told of the adventure was devoid of details until White met an engineer named Dr. C. C. Parry, who was performing a railroad survey in the area. Parry apparently convinced White that he had taken a more substantial journey than he actually had.

All we know for sure is that on September 8, 1867, several individuals spotted a delirious, half-clothed, badly sunburned, and terribly emaciated 27-year-old man on a crude wooden log raft on the Colorado River near Callville, Nevada. White claimed that he and his colleagues were prospecting for gold when they were attacked by Indians and forced to use the river as a route of escape. Where the men were at the time of this Indian attack—and thus the beginning of their journey—is of course the crux of the story and the point on which its veracity hangs.

After his rescue in Callville, White recounted that on August 24—two weeks earlier—one of his colleagues, a "Captain Baker," was immediately killed by the Indians, and that he and his other colleague, George Strole, grabbed their guns, a hank of rope, and several pounds of flour and ran for the river. There they were fortunate enough to find four cottonwood logs four inches in diameter and ten feet long from which they quickly fashioned a raft.

According to White, Baker was immediately killed by the Indians. After three days on the river, Strole was washed off the raft, never to be seen again. Soon afterward, the flour was lost or rendered inedible. White recounted that he then met several Indians, with whom he traded the hindquarter of a dog (which he subsequently ate) for his revolver. White then claimed that he continued downstream for another ten days, lashing himself to the logs to keep from being washed off, before he arrived at Callville—a journey of about 550 miles.

Most of those familiar with the river are skeptical of White's story. Lewis R. Freeman, author of *The Colorado River* and *Down the Colorado*, found the idea "laughable" that someone could travel more than 500 miles on a crude log raft in just two weeks through some of the most treacherous whitewater in America.

As for White's statement that he lashed himself to the raft to keep from being thrown off, Freemen remarked: "I can think of no more certain preliminary to inevitable suicide than such an action—that thus bound he could have survived one major rapid of the Grand Canyon is hardly possible."

Many think White made up the story for the sake of his own glory, while others think he was simply confused and then duped by others. The more suspicious speculated that White killed his two companions and concocted an alibi to explain their disappearance.

Yet a number of individuals still believe the story to be true. The legend of James White has persisted in the annals of the West, along with the claim that it was White, not Powell, who was the first to pass through these wild and remote chasms.

The naysayers have prevailed. Chief among them was Robert Brewster Stanton, who, in his finely wrought book *Colorado River Controversies*, explained: ". . . every one of the actual navigators of the Colorado has refused to believe in the White claims. As one of them, I had always been decidedly incredulous of the serious claim that anybody had succeed in traveling on a raft more than five hundred miles on what is possibly the most dangerous river in the world. And as for the low stage of water having any effect in minimizing the peril, I knew only too well that there are on the river two hundred rapids which are actually many times more dangerous at low water than high."

Stanton concluded: "I had investigated the whole matter with the utmost thoroughness, with the result that I was thoroughly convinced that it was unfounded in fact. As early as 1892 I set forth my position in the matter: Major Powell's expedition of 1869 was undoubtedly the first, and I, having successfully concluded a survey of all the canyons of the river in 1889 and 1890, lay claim to the distinction of being second down the great river."

There were, it appeared, three conflicting accounts of White's journey: (a) the simple letter that White penned to his brother shortly after the trip; (b) the account of Dr. C. C. Parry, who spoke with White and later wrote a report; and (c) an analysis of the story and an interview of White himself.

The letter that White wrote to his brother a few days after the incident is reproduced below in legible (and more literate) language than the original correspondence:

Callville, September 26, 1867.

Dear brother:

It has been some time since I have heard from you. I got no answer from the last letter I wrote you, for I left soon after I wrote. I went prospecting with Captain Baker and George Stroll in the San Juan mountains. We found very good prospects, but nothing that would pay. Then we started down the San Juan River. We traveled down about 200 miles; then we crossed over on the Colorado and camped. We laid over one day. We found that we could not travel down the river, and our horses had sore feet. We had made up our minds to turn back when we were attacked by fifteen or twenty Ute Indians. They killed Baker, and George Stroll [sic] and myself took four ropes off our horses, an axe, ten pounds of flour and our guns. We had fifteen miles to walk to the Colorado. We got to the river just at night. We built a raft that night. We sailed all that night. We had good sailing for three days; the fourth day George Stroll was washed off the raft and drowned, and that left me alone. I thought that it would be my time next. I then pulled off my pants and boots. I then tied a rope to my waist. I went over falls from ten to fifteen feet high. My raft would tip over three or four times a day. The third day we lost our flour, and for seven days I had nothing to eat except a raw-hide knife cover. The eighth day I got some mesquite beans. The thirteenth day I met a party of friendly Indians. They would not give me anything to eat, so I gave them my pistol for the hind parts of a dog. I had one of them for supper and the other for breakfast. The sixteenth day I arrived at Callville, where I was taken care of by James Ferry. I was ten days without pants or boots or hat. I was sun-burnt so I could hardly walk. The Indians took seven head of horses from us. I wish I could write you half I underwent. I saw the hardest time that any man ever did in the world, but thank God that I got through it safe. I am well again, and I hope these few lines will find you all well. I send my best respects to all. Josh, answer this when you get it. Direct your letter to Callville, Arizona. Ask Tom to answer that letter I wrote him several years ago.

[Signed by James White]

Dr. C. C. Parry, who claimed he was a geologist on the 1867–68 railway survey under the supervision of General William J. Palmer (it turns out Parry was a medical doctor and the survey's botanist), met White and prepared a report about his journey. The lengthy title of the report was "Account of the Passage of the Great Canyon of the Colorado, from above the mouth of the Green River to the head of Steamboat Navigation to Callville, in the months of August and September, 1867, by James White, now living in Callville."

Parry attributed to White a more detailed statement than White had previously provided. In his report, Parry concludes: "Now, at last, we have a perfectly authentic account of the character of the Great Canyon of the Colorado, derived from the lips of a man who actually traversed its formidable depths, and who, fortunately for science, still lives to detail his trustworthy observations of this most remarkable voyage."

According to Parry's report, White and two other men were searching for gold in the tributaries of the San Juan River in southwestern Colorado. The three men followed the stream until they reached the Grand River before its meeting with the Green. They camped in a ravine on the night of August 23, and the next day they were climbing the bank when they were attacked by Indians. Captain Baker, the first in line, was killed immediately. White and Strole fought their way back into the canyon, hastily unpacked their horses, and ran down the canyon to the banks of the Grand River. There they quickly constructed a raft of driftwood, secured together with lariat ropes, and pushed away at midnight on the river.

The next morning, August 25, they repaired the raft and continued down a river flowing at what White guessed was two and a half to three miles an hour. About 30 miles later, he claimed, they arrived at the juncture of the Grand and the Green. In another 40 miles, White said, they reached the confluence of the San Juan River. From this point on, the canyon was continuous, with only small side canyons breaking the continuity.

On the fourth day, August 28, White and Strole encountered their first rapids. Strole was washed off the raft and perished in a whirlpool. Without any provisions, White entered what he called "Big Canyon," which consisted of a succession of rapids and boulders. To stay on top of the raft, White lashed himself to it. The next seven days he survived without any food until he finally reached the settlement of Callville, Nevada, on September 8.

Interestingly enough, Parry's report never mentioned the knife sheath or the dog that Perry allegedly ate, according to White's letter to his brother. Parry concluded, rather remarkably, that White's story "bears all the evidence of entire reliability, and is sustained by collateral evidence, so that there is no room to doubt that he actually accomplished the journey in the manner and within the time mentioned by him." Parry, who may have been trying to impress his superiors, undoubtedly went too far when he stated that his was a "remarkable journey" that added to "our previous geographical knowledge of the hydrology of the Colorado."

Robert Brewster Stanton was not convinced. He found it telling that White never mentioned the Grand (now the Colorado), Green, San Juan, or Little Colorado Rivers in his original letter to his brother, nor did he mention the word "canyon" or anything about the height of the surrounding walls. White also claimed there was only one large rapid in the course of the 550 miles he had navigated.

Stanton was persuaded that those surrounding White, particularly Dr. Parry, had convinced him that he had traveled through the Grand Canyon. The power of suggestion prevailed, and there was no malice on White's part.

Stanton sought out White to interview him, and he agreed to do so if paid the sum of $25 beforehand. With the skill of a seasoned trial lawyer, Stanton cross-examined White. As White spoke, several glaring errors appeared in his testimony.

White said it was about 40 miles from the confluence of the Green and Grand to the mouth of the San Juan River; it is actually 150 miles. White said it took a day to cover that distance, but the journey would have taken four days, according to White's estimate of two and a half miles an hour and 15 hours a day. White described the walls as "white sand rock" that were 300 or 400 feet high— these clearly were not the walls of the Grand Canyon.

In his thorough interview, Stanton asked White about the rapids he encountered:

STANTON: *How many big heavy rapids were there on the Colorado River that you passed in your journey?*

WHITE: *In all the journey there was only one big rapid, the one with the 20-foot fall. All the other rapids were small ones.*

Stanton asked about the geology of the canyons that White passed through:

STANTON: *What was the formation of the walls of the canyon? What kind of rock was it?*

WHITE: *The formation of the walls of the canyon was of sandstone, a light yellowish sandstone, all the way from the Green River to within 150 miles of Callville. It is all the same kind of rock, a white or yellowish sandstone.*

Stanton asked about the height of the walls that White saw:

STANTON: *How high were the walls of the canyon through which you went?*

WHITE: *The walls were 300 or 400 hundred feet high. There were some high walls, maybe, farther back. They were higher where I couldn't see them, but what I saw were 300 or 400 hundred feet high, not over 500 hundred feet.*

Then Stanton asked White a particularly revealing question:

STANTON: *How did you know it was the Green River?*

WHITE: *I did not know it then, but General Palmer [Dr. Parry] told me afterwards it was the Green.*

And likewise, Stanton inquired:

STANTON: *How did you know the river you saw was the Little Colorado?*

WHITE: *General Palmer [Dr. Parry] told me it was.*

Stanton persisted with an even more pointed inquiry:

STANTON: *How high were the walls at the mouth of the Green River?*

WHITE: *They were not so high.*

STANTON: *Are you not aware, Mr. White, of the fact as shown on the*

government maps that the walls of the canyon on the lower part of
the Grand and at the mouth of the Grand are 1,400 feet high?
WHITE: *No! Where we stopped at the mouth of the Green I could*
see all over the mesa.

In a most diplomatic manner—and in a remarkable revelation
to White—Stanton concluded his interview:

STANTON: *Now, Mr. White, I will tell you what I think of all this.*
First, be sure to understand I believe every word you say as to your
personal experiences. I do not doubt your word. As far as you know,
you have told the truth. You were on a raft. You floated down part
of the Colorado, but not where you think you did, or rather where
you were told you did. You have been misled by others. You were
picked up from the raft at Callville in September 1867 in a pretty
demoralized condition. That is a proved historical fact.
. . . But you never went to the Grand River, and you never
floated on a raft through Cataract, Glen, Marble, or Grand
Canyon. The fact is that from the time you struck the San Juan
River at the mouth of the Mancos River, you were lost . . .
WHITE: *Maybe I was!*
STANTON: *. . . You have told the truth as far as you knew, that is,*
as to your personal experiences. And further it has been believed by
some very distinguished men that you murdered your two compan-
ions and told your story in 1867 to cover up your crime.
WHITE: *I didn't kill them.*
STANTON: *No, I know you didn't, and now that I know the truth*
I am going to defend you from both charges.

Despite the overwhelming evidence against it, the White
legend has lived on. Fifty years after White was dragged out of
the river at Callville—May 25, 1917, to be exact—the executive

clerk of the U.S. Senate, Thomas Dawson, presented a 67-page document with the following celebratory title: "The Grand Canyon: an article giving the credit of first traversing the Grand Canyon of the Colorado, to James White, a Colorado Gold prospector, who it is claimed made the voyage two years previous to the expedition under the direction of Maj. J. W. Powell in 1869."

Ironically, the same Congress, just a year later, approved the erection of a monument dedicated to Major John Wesley Powell as the *first* explorer of the Colorado River.

Stanton concluded his investigation thus: "And so, from his own testimony, I conclude that James White never passed through a single mile of the canyons of the Colorado River above Grand Wash Cliff, but that he did float on a raft or rafts on that river in the year 1867 a distance of sixty miles [averaging about four miles per day rather than forty] from a point near the Grand Walsh to Callville, Nevada, where he was stopped and taken off his raft. To Major John Wesley Powell, leader of the expedition of 1869 and 1872, therefore, belongs beyond the shadow of a doubt the honor and distinction of having been the first conqueror of the Colorado River."

In the end, White's story was impossible to reconcile with the geography of the Colorado River. He insisted that the first several days he passed through walls of whitish sandstone before coming to a deep slit of black rock—the canyons walls in the Grand Canyon are undeniably red. It would have been 500 miles from the Grand River to Callville—that would have been an incredible distance to cover in such a short period, especially considering the magnitude of the rapids in Cataract and Grand Canyons.

At any rate, Powell was skeptical of White's claim before he descended the river. One can assume that Powell would have been even more so after he had been down the river and seen its rapids.

PART IV

CATARACT, GLEN, AND MARBLE CANYONS

DAYS 56–81:

JULY 18–AUGUST 12

★ ★ ★ ★

BRIEF TIMELINE

July 17: Confluence

July 23: Cataract Canyon

August 3: Glen Canyon

August 5: Marble Canyon

CHAPTER FIFTEEN

BENEATH CLEAR AZURE SKIES, AND SOME 40 MILES from the mouth of Stillwater Canyon, the Colorado River Exploring Expedition at long last reached the merger of the Green and Grand Rivers, where the currents blended gracefully. To the expedition's eyes, the occasion was almost anticlimactic, and the Grand looked like a mirror image of the Green as it flowed through a canyon of similar depth and character.

The name of the Grand River would later be changed in 1921 to the Colorado as a result of political lobby, even though most geographers believed the Green River was the true source of the Colorado. The combination of the two rivers doubled the depth and velocity of the resulting river as it swirled toward its next chasm, which is now known as Cataract Canyon, with a fierce and threatening intensity. At this point, the party had traveled 54 days and 540 miles from Green River, Wyoming.

The surrounding terrain was exceedingly barren and dismal, with virtually no riverbanks except for a few sandbars scattered here and there, and these were constantly being eroded by the rising and falling water level. At this point, the Major decided to stay in camp for four days in what is now the heart of Canyonlands National Park.

The current of the Grand at the confluence of the Green was sluggish, almost lifeless, and Bradley described the expedition's surprise at what they saw:

> *We were led to expect that it was a rushing, roaring mountain torrent which when united with the Green would give us a grand promenade across the mountains. The rock is the same old stone underlaid for the last 20 miles with limestone containing marine fossils and at the junction of these two is as we can see it (1,000 yards) calm and wide and very much unlike the impossible unpassable succession of foaming and raging waterfalls and cataracts which have been attributed to it. . . . We float in upon a scene never before beheld by white men and by all regarded as dangerous of approach, and the last 75 miles of our journey through a dark calm canyon which a child might sail in perfect safety. Surely men do get frightened wonderfully at chained lions.*

During the expedition's time here, Powell made numerous climbs to higher ground with his brother and Bradley. They spent their time taking accurate measurements of longitude, latitude, and the altitude of the walls. They beheld remarkable vistas—mountains, canyons, cliffs, pinnacles, and buttes extending as far as the eye can see.

Powell described the area as "a wilderness of rock . . . ten thousand strangely carved forms in every direction, and beyond the mountains blending with the clouds." In his journal, Bradley poignantly wrote, with religious overtones:

*Sunday again and though a thousand spires point Heaven-
ward all around us yet not one sends forth this welcome peal of
bells to wake the echoes of these ancient cliffs and remind us of
happier if not grander scenes.*

The hot weather continued to the point where it was extremely
stifling, and the men sought shelter from the sun wherever they
could find it. They did, however, discover one advantage of the
heat: it was too much for the mosquitoes, which had virtually disappeared since Desolation Canyon. In their place was the large
black cricket, providing a constant, but not unpleasant, chirping in
all but the deepest canyons.

The Major and Bradley made an ambitious climb to the top
of the rim, and what they found, 3,000 feet above the river, was
remarkable, as expressed by Powell:

*And what a world of grandeur is spread out before us! Below
is the canyon, through which the Colorado runs. We can trace
its course for miles, and at points catch glimpses of the river.
From the northwest comes the Green, in a narrow, winding
gorge. From the northeast comes the Grand, through a canyon
that seems bottomless from where we stand. Away to the west
are lines of cliffs and ledges of rock—not such ledges as you may
have seen where the quarry-man splits his blocks, but ledges
from which the gods might quarry mountains, that, rolled out
on the plain below, would stand a lofty range; and not such cliffs
as you may have seen where the swallow builds it nest, but cliffs
where the soaring eagle is lost to view ere he reached the summit.*

The two men returned to camp, and Powell saw Hawkins using
the sextant, which Powell remarked is "rather a strange proceeding

for him." When Powell asked what he was doing, Hawkins wryly replied that he was "trying to find the latitude and longitude of the nearest pie." Even in these difficult circumstances, the men had not lost their sense of humor.

Unbeknownst to the expedition, their leisurely life was about to change—for the worse. Downstream from here was Cataract Canyon and arguably the most intense stretch of whitewater along the entire river. The chasm is renowned among modern-day river runners for the panoply of 60 rapids in a short span of 50 miles, many of them very significant forces of nature. The canyon would later be nicknamed by boaters as "The Graveyard of the Colorado" for the many accidents that occurred here, a number of them fatal.

The scenery of bare rock, chiseled by the ages, is an austere one. Regardless of where one looks, there is nothing but sandstone— in various shades of red, yellow, brown, and gray—that has been carved into a multitude of towers, buttes, spires, and pinnacles. The rock face is slashed by deep crevices in all directions.

The water was cold, and the men were wet and hungry. Food supplies were becoming dire. Fish and game were hard to come by, the bacon had gone bad, and the bulkheads of the boats were leaking like sieves. The men salvaged what flour they could by screening it through mosquito netting, as detailed by Sumner:

> But when I came to the commissary I was up a stump. We had about five hundred pounds of flour and a little bacon and dried apples. After examining the flour I found it a miserable mess of green fermentation. There was nothing left to do with it but to sift it through a mosquito netting onto a wagon sheet and let it dry. After Howland and I had sifted it we had but two sacks, presumably two hundred pounds, a not very liberal supply, considering our position and numbers at that date. But as

there was no help for it, we looked the subject square in the face.
There was only a dim hope of replenishing the commissary by
finding some deer or mountain sheep on the way.

The men threw out several hundred pounds of flour—a foolish move, for by proper cooking some of it might have been consumed. Together with the losses of food in the wreck of the *No Name* and other mishaps, their food supply had been reduced from a ten-month supply to two, and they were hardly more than halfway to the end of the journey. At this rate they would starve to death long before they escaped the canyons.

Howland complained to the Major that he should have bought more supplies at the agency. The Major countered the criticism by reminding Howland that he had fallen behind on the mapping.

For the next 12 days, the men—completely drenched and constantly yelling at one another to be heard above the roar of the whitewater—portaged and lined the boats around one rapid after another. Huge boulders had fallen from the cliff walls—great, angular behemoths that rolled down the talus and into the channel of the river—to create rushing chutes, swirling whirlpools, and massive waves complete with breakers and foam. In a span of 40 miles, the river dropped more than 400 feet through a wild and surging maze in a canyon whose walls were confining.

The water boomed and plunged over a sea of rocks. It was a mad, unrelenting flood, and the sound of boulders being rolled downstream by the current was like that of distant thunder. In their struggle to stay alive, the men reached a state of complete exhaustion.

In spite of their weariness, there was no choice but to pursue the path laid out before them. On July 21, the expedition cast off from camp and was quickly carried down the swift torrent. They had not traveled far when two portages were required to avoid a particularly dangerous set of waterfalls. There was a cautionary rationale in their approach to the rapids, as Bradley explained, "We can't run them or rather we don't run many of them, on account of our rations. We are afraid they will spoil and if they do we are in a bad fix."

In the afternoon, the *Emma Dean*, attempting to navigate one of the more forgiving descents, was swamped, pitching Powell and his shipmates into the roaring maw. The men were able to cling onto the boat until they floated into more tranquil waters, where they managed to climb back on board, signaling the boats behind them to land immediately. The others were able to pull safely to shore. The tedious, back-breaking process of portaging the craft and gear consumed the rest of the day.

Three oars were lost with the capsize of the *Emma Dean*, and a search was made among the piles of driftwood for logs large enough in which to make oars. While the oars were being carved, Powell and his brother climbed up the canyon walls to collect gum from pine trees for caulking the leaky boats.

Darkness compelled the party to halt for the night on rocks where the men barely had room enough to lie down, as noted by Bradley:

Made four portages and camp tonight in a place where we can only find sleeping ground by piling up rocks around the edge of the water and then collecting the scanty sand from between the huge boulders. In that way, we have made comfortable beds.

The night was a restless one, with the roar of the river raging around them. There was no respite from the unrelenting force, but the expedition simply could not risk the loss of a boat. A rapid that would take 60 seconds to run required two hours to portage, but they had no choice.

The expedition took all the precautions it could, for the rapids arrived faster and more violent than ever. One rapid led to another and then another and then another. The walls rose to almost 2,000 feet and were nearly vertical in places. They checked the barometers and concluded that an even steeper descent lay ahead.

One fear was always on their mind—that of arriving at the brink of a high waterfall surrounded by sheer walls and no means of retreat.

On July 23, three portages were made. The expedition only advanced five and a half miles in the process, but they were able to avoid a stretch of whitewater where the river dropped 75 feet in less than a mile.

Lining the boats in the powerful waves was also dangerous. It rendered the craft extremely unwieldy, as the current slammed into the bows at a diagonal and often sent the boats out of control into the maw of the rapids. The men then had to let go of the lines or else be pulled into the current.

The next few days the rapids increased in severity and the steep walls climbed higher. The river's currents were hammered to foam by immense boulders in the river. The roar of the whitewater was deafening. Occasionally the boats flew at breakneck speed through clean, clear chutes in the middle of the rapids, and the men found the experience exhilarating.

The heat in the canyon was oppressive—more than 100 degrees. The expedition camped among the red-stained limestone walls that rose thousands of feet. The thin strip of sky overhead was the only break from the closing claustrophobia, and the river roared relentlessly as it surged between the ragged canyon walls.

Powell, his brother Walter, and Bradley explored a nearby side canyon, whose resplendent beauty was aptly described by Powell:

We enter it through a very narrow passage, having to wade along the course of a little stream until a cascade interrupts our progress. Then we climb to the right, for a hundred feet, until we reach a little shelf, along which we pass, walking with a great case, for it is narrow, until we pass around the fall. Here the gorge widens into a spacious, sky-roofed chamber. In the farther end is a beautiful grove of cottonwoods, and between us and the cottonwoods the little stream widens out into three clear lakelets, with bottoms of smooth rock. Beyond the cotton-woods, the brook tumbles, in a series of white, shining cascades, from heights that seem immeasurable. Turning around, we can see through the cleft through which we came, and see the river, with towering walls beyond. What a chamber for a rest-ing place is this! Hewn from the solid rock; the heavens for a ceiling; cascade fountains within; a grove in the conservatory, clear lakelets for a refreshing bath, and an outlook through the doorway on a raging river, with cliffs and mountains beyond . . .

The discussion of the rapids ahead consumed the expedition. It was decided that if the descent was evenly distributed throughout its rapids downstream, the party may have a chance of surviving. But there remained the possibility that the party would enter sheer canyon walls before arriving at a precipitous drop with no place to land. The fear of such a waterfall was enough to keep the men awake as they sat around the campfire under a full moon and fret-ted about what lay ahead.

July 24 was a day of perilous rapids caused by house-sized blocks of stone that had fallen from the talus and were strewn throughout the channel. There was no quiet water, only rushing currents as they plunged against the rocks. These obstructions required four difficult portages, which advanced the party downstream only three-quarters of a mile.

One of the men noticed that there was driftwood 30 feet high on the canyon wall. Sumner replied: "God help the poor wretch that is caught in the canyon during high water."

Powell reflected at the end of the day:

A hard day's work has been done, and at evening I sit on a rock by the edge of the river and look at the water and listen to its roar. Hours ago deep shadows had settled into the canyon as the sun passed behind the cliffs. Now, doubtless, the sun has gone down, for we can see no glint of light on the crags above. Darkness is coming on. The waves are rolling, with crests of foam so white they seem almost to give a light of their own. Nearby, a chute of water strikes the foot of a great block of limestone, fifty feet high, and the water piles up against it and roll [sic] back. Where there are sunken rocks, the water heaps up in mounds or even in cones. At a point where rocks come very near the surface, the water forms a chute above, strikes, and is shot up ten or fifteen feet, and piles back in gentle curves, as in a fountain, and on the river tumbles and rolls.

As night fell, the expedition considered itself lucky to find a small bank with pockets of sand on which they could lie down for a brief rest.

July 25 was another day of limited progress—only three and a half miles downriver. The canyon was narrow and deep, and the currents raged at high velocity through a channel littered with enormous rocks. The work of portaging and lining the boats was incredibly laborious as the men moved in and out of the water, climbed over massive boulders along the bank, lifted the boats and slid them on driftwood skids, tugged and pulled on the boats to move them farther along, and finally shoved the boats with all the strength they could muster into the river again.

The expedition made it through one bad spot and was on to the next, requiring one letdown of the boats after another. It seemed like it would never end.

CHAPTER SIXTEEN

IN THE DEPTHS AND DEEP SHADOWS OF CATARACT
Canyon, the men were constantly wet and shivering, and the cold
air was penetrating. Two of the three boats were leaking badly, and
another oar was lost to the currents. The river continued to move
along at locomotive speed, and the men found the millrace to be a
menacing and constant challenge.

The members of the expedition continued to complain. July
26 was a day taken to repair the boats. Bradley revealed a growing
impatience that was shared by all the men:

> *Another day wasted foolishly. Run 1½ miles and finding a
> later canyon Major wished to land and climb the mountains
> so five of us started on a wild goose chase after pitch [to seal the
> boats] but it was so hot we all backed out except the Major who
> says he climbed the cliff, but I have my doubts.*

The next day the rapids consumed the party with even greater
frequency as the gorge became increasingly narrow. The currents
rushed downstream with terrific force, and the violence of the waves

crashing against boulders was taking its toll on the men. The canyon walls, whose faces were ragged and broken, soared 2,500 feet above, and their ultimate heights were another 1,000 feet beyond that. It was the narrowest chasm the expedition had seen so far.

The men were forced to line or portage almost all the rapids. They nimbly leapt from boulder to boulder downstream as they cajoled the boats through the maze of rocks and waves. To maneuver the craft around gigantic boulders away from the shore, they often had to release them into the current and then adroitly reel them back in below the rapids, requiring a tremendous amount of strength, skill, and dexterity.

On July 27 a flock of mountain sheep was discovered on the rocks not more than a hundred feet overhead, and two fat sheep were soon added to the group's rapidly diminishing larder. Sumner called it "a Godsend to us, as sour bread and rotten bacon is poor diet for as hard work as we have to do."

Powell described the group's now-desperate hunt for food:

We quickly land in a cove, out of sight, and away go all the hunters with their guns, for the sheep have not discovered us. Soon, we hear firing, and those of us who have remained in the boats climb up to see what success the hunters have had. One sheep has been killed, and two of the men are still pursuing them. In a few minutes, we hear firing again, and the next moment down come the flock, chattering over the rocks, within twenty yards of us. One of the hunters seizes his gun, and brings a second sheep down, and the next minute the remainder of the flock is lost behind the rocks. We all give chase; but it is impossible to follow their tracks over the naked rock, and we see them no more. Where they went out of this rock-walled canyon is a mystery, for we can see no means of escape. Doubtless, if we could spare the time for the search, we could find some gulch up which they ran.

We lash our prizes to the deck of one of the boats, and go on for a short distance, but fresh meat is too tempting for us, and we stop early to have a feast. And a feast it is! Two fine, young sheep. We are not for bread, or beans, or dried apples tonight; coffee and mutton is all we ask.

The next day the men were startled by an even more dramatic narrowing of the canyon walls. The chasm was now nearly 3,000 feet deep, and the river surged through its winding corridors, which made it impossible for the men to clearly see the hazards ahead. The crew was hungry and tired, and at the end of the day they pulled off their soaking wet clothes and replaced them with ones not quite as wet. Soon the smell of coffee drifted through the camp.

The constant battle with obstacles littered about the river made the men tense, and as a result they quarreled. The food situation was desperate once again. The rapidly deteriorating boats were a constant concern, and the men climbed the cliffs to find pine trees from which they could collect resin to repair the leaks.

Always the climber, Powell ascended the canyon walls whenever he was given the chance. Scrambling up talus slopes, crawling along ledges, squeezing into cracks, and boosting himself up, Powell emerged finally into what he described as a "wilderness of rock . . . ten thousand strangely carved forms in every direction, and beyond them mountains blending into the clouds."

A particularly explosive scene occurred. The men were portaging the boats, and the ropes accidentally caught Dunn under the arms and came close to drowning him. Dunn managed to catch himself, but in the process he ruined one of the Major's expensive chronometers.

At dinner that evening Sumner mentioned to the Major and Walter that Dunn had come close to drowning in the incident. The Major demanded that Dunn pay $30 for the watch on the spot, and that if he did not, he must immediately leave the party.

Hawkins, who was preparing dinner and out of earshot, was told of this conversation by Sumner. Hawkins immediately confronted the Major, who confirmed the discussion. Hawkins replied that it would be impossible for anyone to leave the canyon at this point. Hawkins tried to calm the situation by telling Powell it was unfortunate the watch was ruined and that he felt that way about a member of his own expedition. The Major rebuffed Hawkins, telling him he had no right to interfere in the matter.

Everyone sat down to eat, and Hawkins, for the first time, refused to serve the Major, as he had done since the beginning of the expedition. Hawkins told Powell that he "will have to come and get his grub like the rest of the boys."

After dinner, Sumner informed Hawkins that the Major had not changed his mind about Dunn. Hawkins told the Major that therefore he, Bradley, and Hall would leave the canyons with Dunn by boat. The Major responded that he would not allow it, and that it would be the ruin of the expedition. In an attempt to settle everyone down, Sumner urged all the men to reconsider and give the Major an opportunity to rethink the matter. The next morning the Major told Dunn he could pay for the watch later.

Unfortunately, relations between the men and the Major worsened. The group came to another set of difficult rapids where it was necessary to line the boats. The group needed a strong swimmer to position himself on the rock to push the boat along, and Powell asked Dunn to do so.

Hawkins explained what happened next:

He [Dunn] made the rock all O.K. and was ready to catch the rope which was supposed to be thrown to him, so he could swing the boat in below, but the Major saw his chance to drown Dunn, as he thought, and he held the rope. That was the first time he had interfered in letting the boats around bad places, and the rope caught Dunn around the legs and pulled him into the current and came near losing the boat.

Dunn held on to the rope and finally regained his footing in water up to his hips. Everyone but Powell was in the water.

Dunn told the Major that if he had not been a good swimmer he and the boat both would have been lost. The Major replied that it would have been but little loss. One word brought on another, and the Major called Dunn a derogatory name. Dunn replied that if the Major was not a cripple he would punch him. Then Walter Powell got into the act, swearing at Dunn and threatening to kill him.

As Hawkins explained:

He [Walter] was swearing and his eyes looked like fire. Just as he passed I caught him by the hair of his head and pulled him back into the water. . . . After I got my hold in Cap's hair I was afraid to let go, for he was a very strong man. He was up in a short time and mad! I guess he was mad!

Cursing wildly, Walter lunged for his gun and threatened to kill Hawkins and Dunn. Hall punched Walter behind the ear and told him to either drop the gun or he would "take off his head." The Major rushed toward them, saying he never thought Hawkins would turn on him. Hawkins wrote about the incident: "I told him that he had gone back on himself, and that he had better help Cap get the sand out of his eyes, and that if he monkeyed with me any more I would keep him down next time."

This was a major turning point in the expedition, according to Hawkins: "Sumner and I had all we could do to keep down mutiny. There was a bad feeling from that time on for a few days. We began not to recognize any authority from the Major."

The severity of the rapids increased downstream, and for a few days the group seemed to be coalescing again until the men started telling stories about encounters with Indians. Someone remarked that Dunn had been quiet about the subject. Walter replied that Dunn did not know much about Indians, and the Major tersely added, "Nor anything else." Sumner reminded the men that Dunn had been wounded four times in skirmishes with the Comanches.

The intensity of the canyon and its torrential river continued. The expedition was burdened by the turmoil of the fierce river, intimidating canyon walls, and a frightening isolation from the outside world. The men had no idea what perils lay below, but they feared an impassable waterfall ahead and formidable rapids behind, creating a virtual deathtrap.

The radiance of the chasm was undeniable. In places the canyon walls seemed to be perfectly perpendicular. Picturesque brooks trickled down narrow canyons. Lazy clouds were flecked with the glow of sunlight. The moon was a globe of dazzling silver, flooding the canyon at night with luminescence.

At long last, the expedition arrived at the end of Cataract Canyon, marked by a sharp bend in the river where hundreds of crags, pinnacles, and towers adorned the top of the wall. The claustrophobic confines of the chasm were gone.

The world opened up and provided to the explorers at least a momentary relief from the stomach-turning anxiety of not knowing what deadly perils lay ahead.

CHAPTER SEVENTEEN

THE GRUESOME 50 MILES OF CATARACT CANYON—along with its 60 or so rapids and a very dramatic descent of 400 feet—were now behind the expedition.

The group had descended about 2,600 feet since leaving Green River Station, which was 600 miles and two months away. The men's tattered clothes, disintegrating shoes, and sunburned bodies revealed the severity of the conditions they had miraculously survived.

A clear blue sky and low bluffs of homogeneous red sandstone greeted the party until it left the gorge. The evening of July 28 was spent beside a creek that entered the barren sandstone from river right and was named the Dirty Devil. It was muddy, alkaline, and undrinkable.

Sumner expressed the thoughts of the men about the stream:

At noon on the eight day on the Colorado (July 28th) we rowed into camp just below a side stream coming in from the north which stinks bad enough to be the sewer from Sodom and Gomorrah, or even hell. I thought I had smelt some pretty bad

odors on the battlefield two days after action, but they were not
up to the standard of that miserable little stream.

As an interesting aside, three of the men took credit for naming
the stream, and there remained a question about how it all came
about. John Cooley, in his book, *Exploring the Colorado*, explains:
"Curiously enough, Bradley credits Powell with the name, 'Dirty
Devil,' Powell credits Dunn, and Sumner credits himself. To add
to the confusion, Hawkins says Powell had referred to Dunn as a
'dirty devil' before they came to the stinking river, which he then
dubbed the 'Dirty Devil,' in reference to Dunn. This makes Bradley's reference to being complimented by the name and to reading
'his whole character' somewhat ambiguous. On first reading one
might assume this is a reference to Powell (if so, it is uncharacteris-
tically critical for Bradley), but it could be a more subtle reference
either to Dunn or to 'The Devil.'"

The next day the expedition floated down a quickening current and numerous shoals through low red walls. By any other
standard, the rapids were substantial in size and complexity, but
the men were now experienced in the ways of the river and had
no trouble negotiating them. The walls of the canyon frequently
overhung the river in its bends. Smooth but irregular shapes of
orange rock were stained by iron, giving them an unusual tap-
estry effect. Much of the sandstone contained large potholes,
and some of these contained clear water, which the party took
advantage of.

The expedition soon encountered the remains of an old pueblo
built long go by the Hopi Indians—thin sandstone slabs along
with numerous pottery shards. They estimated them to be at least
200 years old. Sumner reflected: "How they contrived to live is a

mystery to me, as the country around is as destitute of vegetation as a street." Bradley stated that he "would like very much to find one of their villages along the river for they are a hospitable people and retain more of their former customs of the old race than any other living tribe."

Powell the ethnologist had his own theories about the disappearance of the Ancient Ones:

> *At one place, where there is a vertical wall of ten or twelve feet, I find an old, rickety ladder. It may be that this was a watchtower of that ancient people, whose home we have found in ruins. On many of the tributaries of the Colorado, I have heretofore examined their deserted dwellings. Those that show evidences of being built during the latter part of their occupation of the country are, usually, placed on the most inaccessible cliffs. Sometimes, the mouths of caves have been walled across, and there are many other evidences to show their anxiety to secure defensible positions. Probably the nomadic tribes were sweeping down upon them, and they resorted to these cliffs and canyons for safety.*

The river slowed considerably, and the broad, shallow waterway often required the men to disembark from the boats and push their hulls into deeper current. The orange sandstone walls were occasionally cut by narrow side canyons, which in turn led to larger amphitheaters that were domed and resembled caves. Within many of these side canyons were alcoves filled with a variety of trees and shrubs.

On July 30, the party anticipated arriving at the next major landmark, the San Juan River, but the crude map they had brought from Washington was incorrect. They reached the confluence with the San Juan the next day as they rowed against strong headwinds. As expected, it was dirty and desolate. The temperature was well over 100 degrees. The steep and smooth sandstone walls, ranging from 300 to 800 feet high, made it difficult to find a landing spot for the boats.

Sumner suggested they camp in order to correct Howland's topographical work, which he said was somewhat "confused." He also remarked in his diary that the tension between Howland and the Major continued: "Here occurred anther spat between him [Howland] and Major Powell. Will it ever cease?"

Two miles downstream from the San Juan was the now-famous and very dramatic formation known as Music Temple. Here was an entrance through a narrow gorge that widened into a large chamber that was hundreds of feet in diameter. The upper walls arched overhead 200 feet with a narrow swath of sky above. At the back of the enticing grotto was a pool of clear water surrounded by a verdant array of cottonwoods, ferns, moss, and honeysuckle.

Powell commented on their time here:

Here we bring our camp. When "Old Shady" [Walter Powell] sings us a song at night, we are pleased to find that this hollow in the rock is filled with sweet sounds. It was doubtless made for an academy of music by its storm-born architect; so we name it Music Temple.

The first day of August arrived, and as usual, the party was thinking of food. They were down to 15 pounds of bacon, and in a few days they would have nothing other than flour, coffee, and dried apples. The sheep they spotted on the cliffs were worthy of a good meal, but were very elusive, as explained by Bradley:

> *Just saw three sheep this A.M. but failed to get one of them. The rocks are so smooth it is impossible to follow them for they can run right up the side of a cliff where no man can get no foothold. Their feet are made cupping and the outer surface of the hoof is as sharp as a knife. They seem to have no fear of falling but will leap from rock to rock, never stumbling nor slipping though they will be a thousand feet above us and a single missstep would dash them to atoms.*

The canyon walls, almost vertical in places, were exquisite. Small strips of sand lined the banks and were covered with graceful willows. Here the men often found glens and alcoves carved out of the rock, and these were sometimes full of box elder and cottonwoods reflected in the deep pools of water, with sunlight streaming from the bright blue sky above.

The next day the men were relieved from their hunger pains after killing a fat sheep. The canyon walls were low, and the temperature continued to scorch. A well-beaten trail, horse tracks, skeletons of cattle, and campfire rings indicated the previous presence of Indians. The river was completely serene. Because the sandstone formations tended to form mounds and monuments, the Major decided to name it Glen Canyon:

> *The features of this canyon are greatly diversified. Still vertical walls at times. These are usually found to stand above great curves. The river, sweeping around these bends, undermines the cliffs in places. Sometimes, the rocks are overhanging; in*

*other curves, curious, narrow glens are found. Through these
we climb, by a rough stairway, perhaps several hundred feet, to
where a spring bursts out from under an overhanging cliff, and
where cottonwoods and willow stand, while, along the curves
of the brooklet oaks grow, and other rich vegetation is seen, in
marked contrast to the general appearance of naked rock. We
call these Oak Glens. . . .*

*On the walls, and back many miles into the country, num-
bers of monument-shaped buttes are observed. So we have a
curious ensemble of wonderful features—carved walls, royal
arches, glens, alcove gulches, mounds, and monuments. From
which of these features shall we select a name? We decide to call
it Glen Canyon.*

*Past these towering monuments, past these mounded bil-
lows of orange sandstone, past these oak-set glens, past these
fern-decked alcoves, past these mural curves, we glide hour
after hour, stopping now and then, as our attention is arrested
by some new wonder . . .*

The dramatic cliffs in Glen Canyon had been eroded into count-
less shapes and forms. The rock shelters along the orange and red
walls took on an astounding range of natural bridges, windows,
panels, and blind arches.

Considered by many to be the most beautiful chasm along the
entire Colorado River, Glen Canyon's red walls are known for
their symmetric curves, magnificent arches, and the deep, wavy
reflections cast upon the water. Unfortunately, the river in Glen
Canyon is no more, as these magical chasms were inundated by the
waters of Lake Powell on September 13, 1963.

The expedition soon encountered a place of historical significance. In November 1776, two Spanish priests named Atanasio Dominguez and Silvestre Vélez de Escalante crossed here on their way back to Santa Fe from the Rio Virgen. The point has henceforth been known as the Crossing of the Fathers—El Vado de Los Padres.

The canyon walls now climbed higher and narrower, allowing the expedition to put in almost 40 miles that day, the last of them through what Powell described as "variegated shades of beautiful colors—creamy orange above, then bright vermilion, and below, purple and chocolate beds, with green and yellow sands." The monsoon season in these canyons—typically August, when massive thunderstorms invade the area—is well demonstrated, and the party experienced several thunderstorms complete with lightning.

The men stopped at the creek coming in from river right known as the Paria River. At this point they had descended almost 3,000 feet from the beginning of the journey. The Mormons later built a ferry here, which became known as Lees Ferry, and which is now the spot where modern-day boaters begin their 200-plus-mile journey down Marble and Grand Canyons.

Trails, ancient camps, and old milling stones for making bread indicated that the place had frequently been used for fording the Colorado over the years.

Sumner was especially concerned about the Indians:

We saw fresh moccasin tracks at various places in the little valley, a fact which set me on the keenest watch to avoid a surprise. Indians rarely attack an unknown enemy unless they can surprise him. We were in no condition for a fight or a foot race. If the reds saw us, as they probably did, they could see plainly enough to satisfy them that to attempt to surprise us would be very hazardous. Accordingly, none showed up.

As it turns out, the Indians would be the least of the expedition's problems. The Powell expedition would soon enter chasms whose whitewater hazards tested their resolve as they struggled against starvation in the most inhospitable of gorges now known as Marble Canyon and Grand Canyon.

CHAPTER EIGHTEEN

THE EXPEDITION NOW ENTERED MARBLE CANYON'S towering and narrow walls, which are actually gray limestone stained with shades of deep red from water oozing down from oxidized, iron-impregnated formations above.

The crystalline rock here is often polished like glass, and mosses and ferns are sometimes found draped in its enchanting indentations. The journey through the chasm is a geological odyssey of stunning proportions, for the farther one moves downstream, the more layers of rock and time are exposed.

The quickened currents pushed the expedition into turmoil once again, as rocks, having fallen from the surrounding cliffs, created large and boisterous rapids. The river's angry tones permeated the canyon, and the roar reverberated back and forth among the ascending cliffs, which were often terraced. The overwhelming impression the scene provides was one of quickly descending into the bowels of the earth.

The bright sun broiled the men's skin until a sudden cloudburst sent sheets of liquid mud pouring over the rims. In every direction was this fantastic sight of roaring water descending the face of the canyon into the depths below.

On August 5, Powell wrote of the magnificent yet intimidating gorge they entered:

With some feeling of anxiety we enter a new canyon this morning. We have learned to observe closely the texture of the rock. In softer strata we have a quiet river, in harder we find rapids and falls. Below us are the limestones and hard sandstones which we found in Cataract Canyon. This bodes toil and danger....

The canyon is narrow, with vertical walls, which gradually grow higher. More rapids and falls are found. We come to one with a drop of sixteen feet, around which we make a portage, and then stop for dinner.

Then a run of two miles, and another portage, long and difficult; then we camp for the night on a bank of sand.

Marble Canyon, like Cataract Canyon above it and Grand Canyon below it, was filled with rapids too numerous to count. If told there would be a time in the future when modern-day boaters would vigorously compete for the right to negotiate these very waves, the members of the Powell expedition would not have believed it.

Bradley wrote on August 5: "Well, I said yesterday that we had learned to like rapids, but we came to two of them today that suit us too well. They are furious cataracts."

The party completed a number of arduous portages around the rapids, and the men complained that it would be faster, easier, and even safer to simply run the rapids. They accidentally punched a hole in *Maid of the Canyon* while lifting her over the rocks, proving that portaging could be just as hard on the boats as the whitewater.

The next day was one of perpendicular cliffs and swift current. The canyon walls were often vertical and climbed to heights of 3,000 feet above the river, and they offered a magnificent array of turrets, forts, balconies, castles, and a thousand other strange and inconceivable formations that foretold mysterious realms yet to come. The chirping of birds was present, and especially curious was the descending crescendo of the canyon wren.

Before noon the expedition heard the canyon roaring downstream, and they nervously clung to its smooth walls until they could see what lay ahead. The river, dark and somber, appeared as though it could go subterranean at any moment. The men were able to find a small foothold on river left where they landed the boats.

They unloaded the boats, carried the gear downstream, and then lined the boats around the fierce breakers. They did this two more times before the day was over. The toll on equipment was significant, as noted by Bradley:

> *Have been in camp all day repairing boats, for constant banging against rocks has begun to tell sadly on them and they are growing old faster if possible than we are. Have put four new ribs in mine today and calked her all around until she is as right again as a cup. Hope it is the last time she will need repair on this trip.*

The Major and Walter spent four hours climbing 2,000 feet to observe the eclipse of the sun, which would allow them to precisely determine the party's longitude. But the clouds moved in and obscured their view. Disappointed, they started to descend to camp, but darkness fell and caused them to lose their way. The rain then started to pour, turning the rising river to a bright shade of red with the earth brought down in the tributaries.

With no other choice before them, Powell and his brother spent the night halfway up the side of the canyon wall, exposed to pelting rain as they waited for the first light of morning to return to the campsite. When they returned, they had no more knowledge about their longitude than when they first began.

The next day, August 8, brought five portages, but the boats were practically empty, so the task went quickly. The men expressed amazement at the finely polished limestone that looked like marble, and that was colored white, gray, pink, and purple, with saffron tints. The name they gave the chasm—Marble Canyon— seemed appropriate.

Marble Canyon, about 65 miles long, is one of the deepest, narrowest, and most majestic chasms in the Colorado. Many of its walls rise vertically from the water's edge, and some 70 rapids are found in its depths. The expedition had another 1,850 feet to descend before it reached Grand Wash and the end of the journey.

The men's clothes were tattered rags that barely covered their sun-baked bodies. Even in these arduous circumstances, the men took time to write in their diaries about the extraordinary beauty they found in these finely polished depths.

A ray of optimism also shone through Bradley's diary:

We are interested now only in how we shall get through the canyon and once more to civilization though we are more than ever sanguine of success. Still our slow progress and wasting rations admonish us that we have something to do. Fortunately we are a happy-go-lucky set of fellows and look more to present comfort than our future danger and as the cook has a fine set of beans cooking with every prospect that his sweating and swearing will issue in an ample breakfast in the morning, we

John Wesley Powell, five years after the expedition

Imposing chasm of
the Colorado River

Inside the depths of the
Grand Canyon

Overlooking the Inner Gorge

Swift currents raging inside the canyon

Looking downstream into Marble Canyon

Horseshoe Canyon on the Green River

Red Canyon on the Green River

Green River's Desolation Canyon

Emma Dean
on the second
expedition

Powell and the chief of the Paiutes

shall make our beds tonight and no doubt sleep as soundly as if surrounded with all the comforts of "happy home" instead of in a cave in the earth.

The expedition then encountered one of the more spectacular sights in the Grand Canyon: Redwall Cavern. They camped underneath the overhang that formed a massive open-faced chamber that could accommodate a crowd of thousands.

August 9 was another day of difficult portages and dozens of rapids, including several of some consequence. The limestone walls continued to rise abruptly at water's edge, and spectacular springs, caves, and alcoves appeared high on the walls above.

Admiring the gorge before them, Powell said the scenery was "on a grand scale," and that the 2,500-foot walls of the canyon were fantastically colored to a fine sheen:

At one place I have a walk for more than a mile, on a marble pavement, all polished and fretted with strange devices, and embossed in a thousand fantastic patterns. Through a cleft in the wall the sun shines on this pavement, which gleams in iridescent beauty.

A magnificent cascade was seen pouring from the polished limestone wall a hundred feet above and surrounded by bright green ferns trembling in the mist. It is named Vasey's Paradise for botanist George Vasey, a friend of Powell. Bradley called it "the prettiest sight of the whole trip," and Major Powell agreed:

Riding down a short distance, a beautiful scene is presented. The river turns sharply to the east, and seems enclosed by a wall, set with a million brilliant gems. What can this mean?

Every eye is engaged, everyone wonders. On coming nearer, we find fountains bursting from the rock, high overhead, and the spray in the sunshine forms the gems which bedeck the wall. The rocks below the fountain are covered with mosses, and ferns, and many beautiful flowering plants. We name it Vasey's Paradise, in honor of the botanist who traveled with us last year [to the Rocky Mountains].

The canyon walls soared higher as the torrent raged downstream. Remarkable buttresses and terraces were seen here. Colossal precipices loomed on all sides. The crew responded to the Major's commands of "right . . . left . . . hard left . . . steady . . . hard on the right . . . pull away from the cliffs now!"

A strong rainstorm invaded the canyon, and the men watched wave after wave of a bright red mud slurry cascade over the canyon walls, which over the eons of time had left them highly polished. The river maintained its impetuous pace downstream with frightening velocity, and the rowers were ever on the alert during the turbulent descent.

On August 10 the party continued on a river filled with dozens of rapids, large and small, which they managed to run successfully. The oarsmen were especially attentive to the powerful lines between the main current and the eddies that moved upstream, which had the ability to turn the boats over if not entered carefully.

At times the men were barely able to maintain control of the craft in the unpredictable waves of the flood. The fearful commotion of rapids surging through the rocks sped the party into the seething, boiling turmoil.

The expedition was forced to portage several rapids. Eager to move downriver, they grumbled that the Major was too cautious, and that they could have negotiated many of the falls they portaged around. In their minds, this would have saved them valuable time, as well as damage to the boats.

The men finally reached the mouth of the Little Colorado River. This was a landmark they had been anticipating once the river suddenly veered to the south. The tributary also served as the arbitrary boundary marking the beginning of the Grand Canyon.

The well-worn path along the Little Colorado revealed that the Anasazi Indians once lived here, as did numerous ruins of their dwellings, pottery fragments, and drawings on the cliffs. Bradley called it "a loathsome little stream, so filthy and muddy that it fair stinks." Sumner agreed, describing it as "a miserably lonely place indeed, with no signs of life but lizards, bats, and scorpions," which, he added, "seemed like the first gates of hell."

The walls soared to 3,000 feet, making escape virtually impossible. The men killed three rattlesnakes that day. The Major left the group to explore an old Indian trail and did not return until dark, which Sumner criticized as "foolish, to say the least," pointing out that the group was in the thick of Apache and Havasupai country.

The men ended up spending several days in a camp full of rattlesnakes in order to make repairs to the boats, check their records, and take scientific observations of latitude, longitude, altitude, and height of the canyon walls.

At this point, Bradley made a brief reference to the James White story:

> . . . *it is said that a man went through from here on a raft to Callville [Nevada] in eleven days. If so we have little to fear from waterfalls below. But I place but little reliance on such reports though his story had been published with much show of reason and the Major has seen the man.*

The river had taken a visible toll on the men. Their clothing had been reduced to shreds, and their saturated leather shoes had turned to mush. Yet a trace of optimism and patience shone through, with Bradley remarking:

We are sorry to be delayed as we have had no meat for several days and not one sixth of a ration for more than a month, yet we are willing to do all that we can to make the trip a success.

Suddenly, the mood of the party changed for the worse, as shown in Bradley's diary entry on August 11:

The men are uneasy and discontented and anxious to move on. If the Major does not do something soon I fear the consequences, but he is contented and seems to think that biscuit made of sour and musty flour and a few dried apples is ample to sustain a laboring man. If he can only study geology he will be happy without food or shelter, but the rest of us are not afflicted with it to an alarming extent.

The expedition reached a critical crossroads, and at times their leader seemed blissfully unaware of it.

THE GRAND CANYON

DAYS 82–99:
AUGUST 13–30

★ ★ ★ ★

BRIEF TIMELINE

August 13: Grand Canyon
August 25: Lava Falls
August 28: Desertion of Three Men
August 30: Grand Wash Cliffs

CHAPTER NINETEEN

LEAVING THE LITTLE COLORADO RIVER BEHIND them, the members of the Powell expedition were absolutely certain of one thing: they were entering a canyon more dramatic and perilous than any they had seen before.

The summits surrounding them loomed 6,000 feet above the river and were often miles away. The collage of lofty mesas, buttes, and pinnacles overwhelmed the men with its remarkable grandeur. The enormous gorge they traversed was one eminently befitting the name they bestowed upon it: the *Grand* Canyon.

In his book *The Emerald Mile*, Kevin Fedarko describes the challenges facing the expedition: "From the moment they entered the Grand Canyon, the walls rose higher, the space between them narrowed, and the scale of everything shifted. By the end of the first day, several layers of limestone and sandstone had pushed out of the shoreline next to the river and shouldered the rimrock a quarter of a mile into the sky. As each stratum stripped back from the next in a stairlike progression, the entire ensemble began to take on the contours of a giant wedding cake of rock. By the third day, the walls displayed a horizontally banded palette of some half a dozen colors that ranged from tawny gold to deep maroon and later, a rose-petal pastel that seemed to smolder with an inner fire, as if it bore the reflected glare of a furnace deep inside the earth. As the boats penetrated farther into this labyrinth, the cliffs were sculpted into dimensions that were both breathtaking and sublime."

As the expedition hastened its way downriver, the Colorado was increasingly studded by enormous boulders and deep holes in the rushing current. The steep, forbidding walls hemmed in the party as the river became narrower and its swirled currents more and more tortured. A deep, sullen roar raged downstream almost constantly, and at times the entire river seemed to vanish from sight. Its furious waves were beaten to foam as they plunged and boomed ever onward.

Powell described the imposing depths of the canyon:

The walls are about three thousand feet high—more than half a mile—an altitude difficult to appreciate from a mere statement of feet. The ascent is made, not by a slope such as is usually found in climbing a mountain, but is much more abrupt—often vertical for many hundreds of feet—so that the impression is that we are at great depth; and we look up to see but a little patch of sky.

It was August 13, and the expedition had been on the river for 82 days. They were of course unaware of it, but they were only 17 days (and some 200 miles) away from the end of a journey that seemed like it would never end.

The strain on the men was becoming unbearable. Extreme exhaustion, shrinking supplies of food, quickly deteriorating boats, brutal heat, and a cataclysm of whitewater were to blame. The men now viewed the canyon as a prison that must be escaped, and the ordeal became nothing more than a battle for survival. Steep, ragged granite walls rose on both sides as the tumultuous currents lashed and pounded against the deteriorating craft.

The Major described the precarious situation they faced:

We are now ready to start on our way down the Great Unknown. Our boats, tied to a common stake, are chafing each other, as they are tossed by the fretful river. They ride high and buoyant, for their loads are lighter than we could desire. . . .

We are three-quarters of a mile in the depths of the earth, and the great river shrinks into insignificance, as it dashes its angry waves against the walls and cliffs, that rise to the world above . . .

We have an unknown distance yet to run; an unknown river yet to explore. What falls there are, we know not; what rocks beset the channel, we know not; what walls rive over the river, we know not.

On top of it all, the expedition was unsure of its geographical location. Donald Worster, in his book *A River Running West*, explains: "They knew the location of Callville, the Mormon settlement that marked the beginning of the 'known,' and they could figure out where it was in straight-line distance and in change of elevation. What they could not know was how many more turns the river made before reaching that point, or how many rapids it went through, or how many days of portaging and lining they had ahead of them, or whether their victuals would see them through."

The men could not help but notice that the texture of the rock was changing dramatically. The strata of limestone and sandstone started to angle sharply upward in an ominous way that foreboded even bigger rapids and waterfalls ahead. The river—now deep inside the earth—narrowed into a tight, swift channel as large, angry waves slapped against the canyon walls and the boats.

So immense was the scene that Powell called the rapids "puny ripples" when viewed from the rim, and the men "but pigmies, running up and down the sands, or lost among the boulders."

The canyon had overwhelmed the expedition, and they sensed that it was suffocating them. The menacing current, flowing broad and powerful, flung itself downstream with unrestrained force. Only a thin ribbon of sky separated the canyon rims above.

Of the hazards they faced, Bradley wrote, "The rapids are almost innumerable, some of them very heavy ones full of treacherous rocks." The canyon walls became increasingly sheer and the cataracts more ferocious. The men had to frequently unload the boats and line them down to the foot of the rapids in icy cold water, followed by arduous portages of gear. It was such grueling work that the considerable risk of running the whitewater chaos seemed preferable, even though they were terrified by the thought of what lay ahead.

The angry tumult of the Colorado drowned out even thought, and with the roar of the river always in their ears, the men slept fitfully at night. To make matters worse, Powell warned that granite formations would soon appear, and with them even more ferocious conditions. Bradley was confident that circumstances could not get any worse, and he wrote, "I am convinced that no man has ever run such rapids on a raft . . . no rocks ever made can make much worse rapids than we now have."

Sumner was reminded of the James White story:

Camped on the north side at the head of a rapid about 1 mile long with a fall of 50 or 60 feet that has about 100 rocks in the

*upper half of it. How anyone can ride that on a raft is more than
I can see. Mr. White may have done so but I can't believe it.*

Camp that night was pitched in plain view of a boulder-filled
chute that dropped 50 or 60 feet in a mile. The next day the boats
reached the tops of the 15-foot waves, with the breakers engulf-
ing them. The boats were soon sloshing full of water, and new
rapids roared downstream. Powell constantly yelled, "Bail for
your lives!"

Canopies of foam flew furiously into the air as they crashed into
the enormous black rocks in the riverbed. The boats leapt half their
length out of the water before burying themselves on the next dive
into the waves. The men took advantage of the eddies whenever
they could to rest for a moment and bail out the boats before the
next round of whitewater began.

The rapids that followed presented a solid wall of standing
waves, and the hulls of the boats hung for an instant at the top of
the slack water and then plunged into the maelstrom with astonishing speed before disappearing from sight.

When it all seemed hopeless, it started to rain, causing the river
to rise. Darkness filled the gorge, and the waterlogged boats moved
even more sluggishly in response to the oars. Sumner was grim
about the predicament they faced:

> *We were weakened by hardships and ceaseless toil for twenty
> out of twenty-four hours of the day. Starvation stared us in the
> face. I felt like Job: it would be a good scheme to curse God and
> die, but, like him, I did not do it.*

Frustrated, the men directed much of their irritation toward
Powell. Sumner made it clear that the morale of the party was

quickly falling apart: "Major Powell spent the following day geologizing, as he was a nuisance in the work of portaging. His imperious orders were not appreciated. We had troubles enough with him."

Campsites were few and far between, and the men were often forced to sleep on the rocks, making rest difficult. Driftwood for campfires was scarce, and the men, wet and exhausted, had trouble staying warm. Substantial damage to equipment occurred: two oars broken in half and the side of the *Emma Dean* split wide open.

August 14 was a day the Colorado River Exploring Expedition would never forget. Bradley described it as "emphatically the wildest day of the trip so far." Sumner agreed that the day they had survived was a memorable one, noting somewhat humorously that the expedition "finally encountered a stretch of water and canyon that made my hair curl."

One by one, the oarsmen tackled the whitewater hazards as they were stacked like cordwood before them. As each boat pushed off from shore, its bow was immediately grabbed by the forceful current. The men used all their might to stay clear of the enormous rocks rising out of the dark, oily river.

The party was swept downstream in continuous rapids broken by steep falls in the river. In negotiating one particularly dangerous rapid, the *Emma Dean* was immediately filled to the brim with water, but the crew managed to prevent the unwieldy boat from careening out of control and overturning.

The *Maid of the Canyon* was next. The first wave struck her bow with such a powerful force that a capsize seemed inevitable. But the river gods were merciful this time and allowed her through. The *Kitty Clyde's Sister* likewise narrowly escaped disaster, and the men attributed their survival to sheer luck.

Much of the day was spent lining and portaging the quickly disintegrating boats, and the expedition had only six miles of progress to show for it. Grousing continued among the men about the Major's overly cautious attitude, and Bradley argued for a more aggressive approach:

> *We have lowered the boats to this point by clinging to the side of the cliff and working them along as best we could. It injures them very much and if I could have my say we should run it for the risk is no greater and we can run it in a few moments while this will take us nearly another half day.*

The canyon walls were closing in, and the river now dropped dramatically out of sight with a vengeance. The men estimated that the waves were 15 feet high in places. Should they risk running it?

Sumner was now in charge of the whitewater logistics due to what he called "the petty quarrels" between Powell and the Howland brothers and Dunn. He decided to choose the river over the land:

> *A fall below meant certain destruction to all. I stated the case and asked, "Who follows?" I can still hear the ringing voices of Hawkins and Hall: "Pull out! We'll follow you to tidewater or hell!" Carefully fastening the hatches and directing the other boats to keep a hundred yards apart, I started out. The* Emma Dean *had not made a hundred yards before an especially heavy wave struck her and drove her completely underwater. Though it did not capsize her or knock anyone out, the wave rendered her completely unmanageable. Dunn and I laid out all our surplus strength to keep her off the rocks, while Major Powell worked like a Trojan to bail her out a little.*

Sumner described the perilous fate of the other boats that followed in their wake:

> *The other boats had disappeared around a curve, and had encountered we knew not what. Giving the* Emma Dean *all the speed we possibly could, we passed through the rapid, ducked at every wave, but as we struck them just right we did not fill. After half a mile of such work we caught up with the other boats, landed in a quiet cove. They greeted us with a ringing cheer as we rounded in.*

After a long day of battling rapids and portaging boats, the group was forced to sleep among the boulders along the shore because there was no riverbank. The greatest fear was that one of them would roll into the river, but they managed to survive a sleepless night without incident. Bradley elaborated:

> *We have but poor accommodations for sleeping tonight. No two except Major and Jack can find space wide enough to make a double bed and if they don't lie still we shall "hear something drop" and find one of them in the river before morning. I sleep in a wide seam of the rocks where I can't roll out. Andy has his bed just above the water on a fragment at the water's edge scarce wide enough to hold him. The rest are tucked around like eve-swallows wherever the cliff offers sufficient space to stretch themselves with any degree of comfort or safety.*

The next day, August 15, the wooden boards of the boats were so water sodden they were the consistency of wet cardboard. The men carefully lowered the frail *Emma Dean* onto several large boulders, and its sides nearly collapsed. Bradley and Walter Powell loaded the boat's gear into the *Maid of the Canyon* and decided to take their chances on the river.

Once in the current, they virtually flew through the milieu of dangerous rapids before they found themselves circulating in the whirlpools below. They headed for shore and entered an eddy just in time to see *Kitty Clyde's Sister* make the run. Hawkins and Hall entered the rapids a little too close to the wall and broke an oar. Sumner recounted the incident:

> *Through hard usage all the boats were getting short on oars. We therefore looked anxiously for a drift log to make them from. The river is so terrific is seems to smash everything into pieces, leaving nothing large enough to make an oar.*

That night they camped on a sandy beach near a clear stream they called Silver Creek (later renamed Bright Angel Creek, perhaps as an accommodation to Dirty Devil Creek upstream). They hiked up the stream and found a number of red spruce logs and began the process of making oars from scratch.

Another calamity occurred the next day: Oramel Howland lost his notes, as well as the map of the river extending from the Little Colorado to this point, when they were washed overboard in the rapids. The incident was a reminder of how a small mishap could have egregious consequences, like the accident that befell Hawkins when he spread out all the rations to dry while making dinner that night. His boat was swung around by an eddy, and the bow line caught the box of baking soda lying on the ground and dragged it into the river. The loss forced the men to eat unleavened bread for the remainder of the trip.

Tuesday, August 17 saw three more portages, one of which badly damaged the *Maid of the Canyon* when her bow struck a rock, requiring considerable repairs. The last portage consumed most of the afternoon, and after it was completed, the river dropped into another series of impassable rapids. Rather than start another portage, the men called it a day, set up camp, and went hunting.

The day's efforts had resulted in relatively little progress—less than ten miles. Supper, as usual, consisted of a small piece of unleavened bread.

The next day was worse. The fearful waves came from all directions at once and tossed the boats wildly about, filling them half full. The party only advanced four miles. Enormous side canyons appeared, and the huge boulders they spewed into the main current littered the flow with formidable obstacles.

Bradley wrote of the group's starvation and exhaustion as they struggled their way downstream:

> *If we could we would run more of them because our rations are not sufficient to anything more than just to sustain life. Coffee and heavy bread cannot be called light rations but one feels quite light about the stomach after living on it after a while. We have just lowered our boats over a very treacherous rapid and camped at its foot, for just below us is another all ready to start on in the morning with a fine chance for a man to see what strength he has gained by a night's rest.*

Whirlpools spun the boats around with abandon, and the strenuous portages slowly sapped the men's strength. Powell wrote on August 18, after a day full of portages and only two miles of progress downstream:

> *While the men are at work making portages, I climb up the granite to its summit, and go away back over the rust-colored*

sandstones and greenish yellow shales, to the foot of the marble wall. I climb so high that the men and boats are lost in the black depths below, and the dashing river is a rippling brook; and still there is more canyon above than below. All about me are interesting geological records. The book is open, and I can read as I run. All about me are grand views, for the clouds are playing again in the gorges. But somehow I think of the nine day's rations, and the bad river, and the lesson of the rocks, and the glory of the scene is but half seen.

The Powell expedition found itself in an untenable position—surrounded by dark canyon whose walls heaved their way straight up toward the heavens, and a menacing river whose broad and powerful currents seemed destined to undo them. And all with absolutely no means of retreat.

CHAPTER TWENTY

THE POWELL EXPEDITION NOW ENTERED WHAT IS ominously known as the Inner Gorge of the Grand Canyon. Here the fierce, tossing waves rushed through the canyon walls so powerfully that the boats could not help but be pulled into them.

Even between rapids, the party flew downstream at a terrifying pace between boulders the size of small houses. Bradley wrote of the incredibly forceful currents that shoved the boats—"whirling and rushing like the wind"—downstream:

The rapid we started with this morning gave us to understand the character of the day's run. It was a wild one. The boats labored hard but came out all right. The waves were frightful and had any of the boats shipped a sea it would have been her last for there was no still water below. We ran a wild race for about two miles, first pulling right— then left, now to avoid the waves and now to escape the boulders, sometimes half full of water and as soon as a little could be thrown out it was replaced by double the quantity.

On August 19, after a portage and lunch in the pouring rain, the men arrived at a particularly furious piece of whitewater. The river dropped away abruptly, then rose again in a succession of fearsome rapids whose crests leaped and danced high in the air. The descents down these waves were exceedingly sharp, and the boats were tossed around like leaves before a storm in a chaos of commotion that almost completely buried them.

The *Emma Dean* swamped immediately in the churning bowels of the river. The other boats tried to assist but were soon thrown against the rocks. By the time its struggle was over, the *Emma Dean* was almost completely underwater. The men jumped out of their boats and towed the *Emma Dean* to shore. Amazingly, nothing was lost but a pair of oars. But the expedition had only advanced six miles for the day.

Adding further hardship was the rain. Donald Worster describes it well in *A River Running West*: "What the torrents of rain did for them was to illustrate exactly how the canyons and rapids had been formed. Water cascaded over the rims, adding to the deafening noise of the river, water carrying mud and silt of various hues. It came plunging down the side canyons with locomotive force, flowing not as clear rainwater but as an avalanche of moving earth, boulders, and trees. Hundreds of tons of loose rock and soil could rumble down in such a debris flow, tearing loose boulders the size of houses and dropping them into the main channel."

Worster continues: "Nothing so terrifying occurred to the Powell expedition, but they could clearly see what had created the rapids that gave them so much trouble. The suddenness with which the river could rise, or the side canyons become a Niagara, or the rocks be covered by a flash flood, or huge boulders loom suddenly in their way made them realize that this was not a place that could be easily learned and mastered once and for all. A single storm could diminish all the expertise they had acquired."

Downstream, the waves broke in a powerful deluge against the bows of the boats. Once through the maelstrom, the men bailed with camp kettles to lighten the craft before they were swept into more rapids whose hazards they could not see from the river.

Sodden to the core, the men strained every muscle they had to pull the boats out of the river. Bradley wrote: ". . . our bedding was so wet we concluded it was best to stay where we were and dry out. So we stayed until noon, had dinner, and then loaded up our boats having dried everything nicely."

On day 90, which happened to be August 21, the cataracts were furious among the towering granite slabs that were scattered along the river. Powell wrote of the awesome millrace ahead:

> *Below, the river turns again to the right, the canyon is very narrow, and we see in advance but a short distance. The water, too, is very swift, and there is no landing place. From around this curve there comes a mad roar, and down we are carried, with a dizzying velocity, to the head of another rapid. On either side, high above our heads, there are overhanging granite walls, and the sharp bends cut off our view, so that a few minutes will carry us into unknown waters. Away we go, on one long, winding chute. I stand on deck, supporting myself with a strap fastened on either side to the gunwale, and the boat glides rapidly where the water is smooth, or striking a wave, she leaps and bounds like a thing of life, and we have a wild, exhilarating ride for ten miles, which we make in less than an hour.*

That night, a beautiful full moon reflected ominously on the canyon walls, Bradley complained, although good-naturedly:

I feel more unwell tonight than I have felt on the trip. I have been wet so much lately that I am ripe for any disease, and our scanty food has reduced me to poor condition, but I am still in good spirits and am threatening all sorts of revenge when I get to decent food once more.

A few days later, Powell described the splendor of a waterfall spewing its beautiful plume from the side of the canyon wall. The water fell in great plunges and vanished in feathery white spray. The sight was quite magical, and the spectacular force of nature was given the poetic name of Deer Creek Falls:

> *Just after dinner we pass a stream on the right, which leaps into the Colorado by a direct fall of more than a hundred feet, forming a beautiful cascade. . . . Around on the rocks, in the cave-like chamber, are set beautiful ferns, with delicate fronds and enameled stalks. The little frondlets have their points turned down, to form spore cases. It has very much the appearance of the Maiden's Hair fern, but is much larger. This delicate foliage covers the rocks all about the fountain, and gives the chamber great beauty.*

The descent downriver continued swift and continuous among perfectly shaped whirlpools and boils in the river. The boats were pushed around like pieces of flotsam, tossed from one side of the river to the other, and spun around and around. The boats were swept uncontrollably downstream beneath dark and sheer walls.

On Tuesday, August 24, after a nice run of some two dozen miles, Bradley suggested to the others that they could not possibly be far away from the end of the journey. The next day, they met the most renowned rapids in the canyon: Lava Falls. The lava extended

1,500 feet up the sides of the canyon, and the falls were signaled by a massive volcanic plug sticking straight up in the middle of the river, now known as Vulcan's Anvil.

Powell's description of the spectacle was suitably dramatic:

> *We make twelve miles this morning, when we come to monuments of lava, standing in the river; low rocks, mostly, but some of them shafts more than a hundred feet high. Going on down, three or four miles, we find them increasing in number. Great quantities of cooler lava and many cinder-cones are seen on either side; and then we come to an abrupt cataract. Just over the fall, on the right side, a cinder-cone, or extinct volcano, with a well-defined crater, stands on the very brink of the canyon. This, doubtless, is the one we saw two or three days ago. From this volcano vast floods of lava have been poured down into the river, and a stream of the molten rock has run up the canyon, three or four miles, and down, we know not how far. Just where it poured over the canyon wall is the fall.*

And Powell then added, "What a conflict of water and fire there must have been here! . . . What a seething and boiling of the waters; what clouds of steam rolled into the heavens!"

The men portaged the boats and gear around the rapids on the south bank. Eager to be off the river, they made 35 miles that day. That evening, the last sack of flour was opened. It was day 94 of the expedition.

CHAPTER TWENTY-ONE

THE MEN COULD NOT HELP BUT NOTICE THAT BLACK granite walls were starting to appear again in the strata of the canyon. This caused them great anxiety. The entrance to the chasm, choked with boulders, required a portage, and the incessant roar of rapids downstream began again.

On August 27 the expedition encountered what Bradley said was "the worst rapid yet seen"—and the crew had seen plenty. Bradley elaborated:

> *The water dashes against the left bank and then is thrown furiously back against the right. The billows are huge and I fear our boats could not ride them if we could keep them off the rocks. The spectacle is appalling to us. We have only subsistence for about five days and have been trying half a day to get around this one rapid while there are three others in sight below. What they are we cannot tell, only that they are huge ones.*

Bradley described the effect of the turbulence on the group's morale, especially in light of their meager food supplies:

There is discontent in the camp tonight and fear some of the party will take to the mountains but hope not. This is decidedly the darkest day of the trip but I don't despair yet. I shall be one to try to run it rather than take to the mountains.

At eleven o'clock that morning, the men arrived at a cataract worse than any they had yet encountered. A thin creek entered the river on the left. They landed first on river right and clambered over the granite pinnacles for a mile or two, but could see no way in which to let the boats down. To run the rapids, they concluded, would be certain death.

After dinner, the party rowed across the river to examine the rapids on the left side. High above the river they walked along on the boulders, but they found it difficult to get a clear view of the river—and the hazards—downstream.

Powell stood precariously on the wall, with one foot secure while clinging with his left hand in a narrow crack in the rock. He then discovered that he was stranded 400 feet above the river, and he called out for help. The men came and threw a rope, but he could not let go of the rock long enough to grab it. They brought several large oars and wedged them into the wall to provide a bridge on which he could walk.

The afternoon was spent scouting the rapids that lay ahead. Side streams had brought tons of loose rock into the river, which at this point dropped almost 20 feet. This turbulence was followed by another long and complicated rapid and then another fall. And there was even more turbulence beyond that.

Powell wrote of his decision to run the rapid:

Then there is a rapid, filled with huge rocks, for one or two hundred yards. . . . I decide that it is possible to let down over the first fall, then run near the right cliff to a point just above the second, where we can pull out into a little chute, and, having run over that in safety, if we pull with all our power across the stream, we may avoid the great rock below. On my return to the boat I announce to the men that we are to run it in the morning. Then we cross the river and go into camp for the night on some rocks in the mouth of the little side canyon.

The expedition, now completely emaciated, faced a rapid that looked utterly hopeless and whose sheer cliffs rendered lining and portaging impossible.

After dinner, Oramel Howland quietly approached Powell to suggest that he and two others—his brother Seneca and William Dunn—would leave if the expedition was not immediately terminated. The only hope for the expedition, Howland explained, was to climb north out of the gorge through the side canyon onto the Shivwits Plateau and then to one of the Mormon settlements.

Certain that the long trek through the desert was suicide, and confident that the group was not far from the end of the journey, Powell displayed to Howland carefully wrought sextant calculations. Howland remained unconvinced, and he and Seneca and Dunn stood firm on their decision to abandon the party. Sumner, Bradley, Hawkins, Hall, and Walter Powell agreed to follow the Major. If there were bitter exchanges, no diary entry records them.

Hawkins wrote:

I have been present at many solemn occasions, but I never witnessed one that came up to this. Some strong men shed tears. Bradley said it made him a child again. We crossed over to the west side of the river and there we left our instruments and

*one boat. This is the last time we ever saw Dunn and the two
Howland brothers alive.*

The men baked the last of the flour and divided the biscuits,
ammunition, and guns in half. Each group carried a set of scientific
notes. The *Emma Dean* was left behind, and the three defectors,
after they helped position the remaining two boats into place for
negotiating the rapids ahead, climbed onto a high ledge to watch
the descent.

The boaters crashed through the waves of the whitewater below
and were soon out of sight. Powell shot off a gun to indicate they
had survived the rapids. The river party pulled to shore, hoping the
three men left behind would change their minds and join them.
But they never did.

The expedition continued through a succession of rapids until
noon, when they arrived at another ugly set of rapids, which they
were forced to line. Bradley remained in one of the boats in order
to fend it off the rocks. The boat started to overturn, and finding
himself in a serious predicament, Bradley cut the line. The stern of
the boat pulled away from shore. Bradley entered the rapids alone,
but he was a powerful man and grabbed an oar, made several strong
strokes, and aimed the bow downstream, where he disappeared
into the foaming waves.

He wrote about the incident later:

*We got a good little run over an almost continuous rapid until
about the middle of the p.m. we came to some more of the lava
and a tremendous rapid. Thinking it possible to let our boats
around by the cliff I got into mine to keep her off the rocks and
the men took the rope (130 feet long) and went up on the cliff
to let her down, not dreaming but what it was a comparatively*

easy task. For a time it worked finely but the cliff rising higher as they advanced and the tide getting stronger as we neared the rapid the task became more difficult until the rope was no longer long enough and they were obliged to hold it just where it was and go back to the other boat for more rope. The water roared so furiously that I could not make them hear and they could not see me, I was so far under the cliff, but where they held me was just on a point of the crag where the tide was strongest. With four more feet of rope I could have got into the tide and then come in with terrible force against the rocks. I got out my knife to cut the rope but hoped relief would come soon, and one look at the foaming cataract below kept me from cutting it and then I was suffering all the tortures of the rack, but having sufficient sense left to look out the best channel through if anything should give way, and it was lucky I did so, for after what seemed quite half an hour and just as they were uniting the two ropes, the boat gave a furious shoot out into the stream. The cut water rope and all flew full thirty feet in the air and the loosened boat dashed out like a war-horse eager for the fray. On I went and sooner than I can write it was in the breakers but just as I always am, afraid while danger is approaching but cool in the midst of it, I could steer the boat as well as if the water is smooth. By putting an oar first on one side and then on the other I could swing her around and guide her very well, and having passed the worst of it and finding that the boat was equal to the task I swung my hat to the boys on the cliff in token of "All's Well."

Bradley had escaped the rapids unharmed. The men who were in his boat had to make a long and difficult climb before they were able to rejoin the group. By evening the party had left the granite formations behind. At noon the next day, they emerged from the depths of the chasm near the mouth of the Grand Wash.

Below this point, Powell was guided by a set of notes that explorer Jacob Hamblin and his party kept on a boat journey several years earlier that extended from Grand Wash to Callville, Nevada. Because Lieutenant Ives and others had traveled up the river as far as Callville, the exploration of the Colorado River was now complete.

A few miles later, the boaters came to the last rapid, which they were prepared to line around. Bradley was still in the boat when the stern line broke free. Bradley rowed furiously to keep the boat from being swept broadside into a vulnerable position in the waves. Sumner and Walter Powell chased him on shore, while the others followed him in the remaining boat, which quickly capsized. Here, in the waning days of the expedition, the Major came as close to drowning as he ever had.

The expedition ended a few days later where the Rio Virgin enters the Colorado. Suddenly gone were the weariness, the hunger, the fear, the personal resentments, the constant anticipation of whitewater hazards downstream, and the physical labor of lining and portaging the boats around waterfalls—all in a barren landscape so forbidding that even the native American tribes of the region had avoided it like the plague.

CHAPTER TWENTY-TWO

ABOUT NOON ON AUGUST 29, THE WALLS OF THE
Grand Canyon opened up and the Powell party could see in every
direction. Sumner called it "a strange and delightful sensation."

The men were elated beyond words, and Walter started singing
in his fine baritone voice. Hall tried to follow suit with his poorly
trained vocal cords, and Hawkins joked that if Hall did not shut
up, he would drown him.

In his journal, Powell waxed both rhapsodic and reminiscent
about the journey now complete: "Now the danger is over, now
the toil has ceased, now the gloom has disappeared, now the firma-
ment is bounded only by the horizon, and what a vast expanse of
constellations can be seen!"

The men saw human footprints and moccasin prints along
the shore. A nude female Indian appeared out of nowhere (as did
a very strange soap-devouring male colleague), as so delightfully
described by Sumner:

*After dinner we ran perhaps three miles. A squaw suddenly
bounced out of some mesquite bushes and cut out down the*

sand at a gait that would have thrown dust in the eyes of Maud S. As she was clothed only in chastity and appeared to have some business down farther, we did not interview her ladyship. A half-mile farther we turned a bend in the river and came to a wikiup with one of Nature's noblemen squatting in front. As we approached the mansion, our Lady Godiva (this one, however, traveled on foot) put in an appearance, evidently to protect her lord. As her first salutation was, "Heap hungry! Towae (tobacco)!" we knew there must be white men in the neighborhood. We tossed the Indians some tobacco and Hawkins threw a cake of fancy-colored soap to one of the papooses. He caught it with the dexterity of a monkey and proceeded to devour it without further ceremony.

The expedition encountered white men who lived nearby and informed them that they had arrived at the mouth of the Virgin River. After resting a few hours, the fishing among the crew began, and Hawkins baked the catch. The Indians looked on with some disdain, as they preferred raw, foot-long lizards. Next arrived a bishop of the Mormon Church and a well-known guide in the area, who brought melons, vegetables, and flour for the men to devour.

Soon the elation of the men who had followed Powell through almost a thousand miles of canyons gave way to disgruntlement. Powell had no interest in navigating the final 600 miles of the river. He gave Sumner, Bradley, Hawkins, and Hall what little money he could spare and the remaining two boats. Bradley wrote in his journal: "After two years [beginning with the field trips in 1867] I find myself penniless and disgusted with the whole thing, sitting under a Mesquite bush in the sand."

Powell's last entry, on day 97, August 28, 1869, revealed the utter fatigue of a journey now complete:

Boys left us.
Run rapids.
Bradley boat broke.
Camp on left bank.

The Powells left the next day with the Mormon bishop for Salt Lake City, and they would eventually travel back to Chicago. The river party was thus reduced to four: Sumner, Bradley, Hawkins, and Hall.

The rest of the group drifted down to Callville, Nevada, where James White was found several years earlier. The group stopped at Camp Eldorado, a mining camp of about 50 men, where, according to Sumner, they had to listen to "that silly story of James White's navigating the Colorado River on a raft." Sumner commented that White "was probably some renegade horse thief that had to leave between two days, and very likely struck the Colorado River at the mouth of the Grand Wash."

The men arrived at Fort Mojave, Arizona, where they were well received and drew four months' supplies of rations. Bradley and Hawkins drifted down to Fort Yuma, and Sumner and Hall rowed all the way to the salt water of the Pacific Ocean, thereby becoming the first to traverse the entire Colorado River system from its headwaters to the sea.

As for the three men who left the expedition, no one knows for sure (their bodies were never recovered), but it was assumed that the Howland brothers and Dunn climbed up the steep cliffs to the summit of the Shivwits Plateau, some 5,500 feet above the river. They undoubtedly traveled northward, where they arrived at a large water pocket, a favorite camping ground of the Shivwits Indians.

Jacob Hamblin of Kanab, Utah, heard the rest of the story from the Utes, who said they welcomed the men at their camp and gave them food. Later that night some of the tribe came into camp and reported certain violations of Ute women by white miners. Several of the Indians assumed it was the three men from the river, and the next morning they were murdered while getting water from the springs. Their guns, clothing, watches, and other scientific equipment were taken by the Shivwits. Of course, it is entirely possible that robbery was the sole motivation for murdering the three men, with the story about the rapes concocted to justify their actions.

In the end, we will never know.

CHAPTER TWENTY-THREE

IN HIS REMARKABLE JOURNEY, MAJOR POWELL showed the world that it was possible to traverse the thousand miles of the Green and Colorado Rivers and the tortuous canyons that punctuated their length, which was clearly an impressive accomplishment.

But the geological and topographic results of the voyage were generally considered to be disappointing, due primarily to the loss of the scientific equipment and the poor notes that were compiled along the way. Powell felt that another survey of the river was called for, and this time the government was more than willing to finance the venture.

Two years later, Powell organized another expedition. He retraced a portion of the 1869 venture, this time with ten other men in a voyage that extended from Green River, Wyoming, to Kanab Creek in the Grand Canyon, when the Major decided that he had had enough. None of the men from the first expedition were among the new crew (Sumner was the only one invited, but he politely demurred). In spite of the shortcomings of the previous boats and the crew's lack of experience, the new expedition used three boats of exactly the same design, with men who had no previous river experience—almost all were relatives or personal friends of Powell's—in spite of the hundreds of applications begging for a spot among the crew.

There were, however, several improvements in the second voyage. For one, every member of the expedition was provided a flotation jacket for safety reasons. Second, heavy rubber sacks were used to protect the valuable food supplies, which were brought into the river at four different points. The new boats featured middle compartments for additional storage, and Powell had a wooden chair firmly attached to the top of his boat so he could more comfortably scout the rapids ahead. Most significant, there was a trip photographer to record the journey and to document the stunning scenery along the way.

The three craft chosen for the second expedition—the *Emma Dean* (once again dedicated to Powell's wife), the *Nellie Powell* (named for Powell's sister), and the *Canonita*—were 22 feet long and constructed of half-inch oak with double ribs). Besides the usual set of oarlocks on the gunwales, a heavy oarlock was attached to the stern to accommodate an 18-foot-long stern oar. The craft were entirely decked over with the exception of the compartments left open for the rowers.

The party pushed off from Green River, Wyoming on May 22, 1871—almost exactly two years to the day after the first expedition. The *Emma Dean* was manned by John Wesley Powell himself, S. V. Jones (a topographer), J. K. Hillers (the photographer), and F. S. Dellenbaugh (an assistant to the geologist and later a topographer). The *Nellie Powell* was rowed by A. H. Thompson (a geographer), J. F. Steward (a geologist), F. M. Bishop (a topographer), and F. C. A. Richardson (an assistant to the geologist and a topographer). The *Canonita* was manned by E. O. Beaman (also a photographer), W. L. Powell (an assistant to John Wesley Powell, his uncle), and A. J. Hatten (a cook).

The men's personal equipment was placed inside rubber sacks, which were then placed inside cotton bags for further protection. Each man was allowed two bags and 100 pounds for clothes, blankets, and other incidentals. In addition, there were some two dozen rubber bags containing more than a thousand pounds of flour.

Frederick Dellenbaugh, Powell's 19-year-old assistant, reported: "We were much better provided for than the first party. We had a guide [trip notes from the previous expedition], our boats were superior, our plan for supplies was immeasurably better, both as to caring for what we took along and what we were to recover at the several indicated places—mouth of the Uinta, mouth of the Dirty Devil, Crossing of the Fathers, and the Paria. We also had better life preservers to inflate at the more dangerous points."

In spite of his youth, Dellenbaugh astutely observed about the river's hazards: "High water makes easy going but increases the risk of disaster; low water makes hard work, batters the boats, and delays progress, but as a rule is less risky." It is a rule followed by today's river travelers. Dellenbaugh also reflected the feeling of modern-day boaters when he wrote that on the river he felt "more than ever a sense of intruding into a forbidden realm, and having permanently parted from the world we formerly knew."

As it turned out, the second Powell expedition encountered no problems in Lodore or Desolation Canyons, as it had before. Cataract Canyon, however, was a different matter. Dellenbaugh wrote: "It was the narrowest chasm we had yet seen, and beneath these majestic cliffs we ourselves appeared mere pigmies, creeping about with our feeble strength, to overcome the tremendous difficulties.

The loud reverberation of the roaring waters, the rugged rocks, the topping walls, the narrow sky, all combined to make this a fearful place, which no pen can adequately describe."

By the time the party arrived at Glen Canyon, the daily rations for each man were extremely low—a thin piece of bacon and a single piece of bread, but plenty of coffee. Every few days a precious cup of bean soup was served. To allow for a faster descent, the *Canonita* was eventually abandoned on the cliffs, and the men made haste downstream.

By the time the expedition reached the mouth of the San Juan, food for only two or three meals remained. Miraculously enough, a fish was caught when they were down to their last morsels.

At the Crossing of the Fathers (present-day Lake Powell) on October 10, the Major traveled overland to Salt Lake City to make provisions for wintering over in the nearby mountains. The rest of the men proceeded downstream some 35 miles to the Paria River, where they cached the boats for the winter.

The following summer, the expedition was back on the river. About 20 miles below Bright Angel a capsize occurred, and Powell came as close to losing his life as he ever had. Expedition member Hillers recalled: "I done some of the tallest kicking I ever done in my life. I thought it an age—all at once I felt myself brought up suddenly, and the next instant I had hold of the gunwale of the boat. Major and myself came up together in a boil. Must have been in the same whirlpool with me, as he spoke of being taken down by one, but he fortunately had his life preserver on or else he might have been drowned, having one arm."

Shortly thereafter, Powell decided to terminate the expedition. Dellenbaugh described the abrupt ending: "The day following our arrival at the mouth of the Kanab Canyon was Sunday, September 8th, and with the exception of some observations taken by Professor [Thompson], and the writing of notes, the whole camp was in a state of rest. After our trying work in the granite we enjoyed immensely the lying around warm and dry with plenty to eat. Monday morning everybody expected to begin preparations for the descent to the Grand Wash. We were surprised just as we were about to rise from our places around the canvas on which breakfast had been spread, when the Major, who was sitting in his chair thinking, suddenly exclaimed, 'Well, boys, our voyage is done!'"

Dellenbaugh explained: "In a way these words were a disappointment, for we all wanted to complete the task and we were entirely ready to go on, notwithstanding that our recent experience with high water in the granite indicated great hazard ahead, where there was more granite; but on the whole the disappointment was agreeable. We knew the second granite gorge toward the lower end of the chasm to be nearly as bad as the first one. There was besides one exceedingly difficult passage there, which Professor [Thompson] called Catastrophe Rapid, where the Howlands and Dunn had left the first party, which on the prevailing stage of water the Major believed would be foolhardy to attempt."

Regarding Powell's hasty retreat from the river, some critics might accuse Powell of the same timidity that allegedly drove the Howland brothers and Dunn overland near this point. But Dellenbaugh and other admirers of Powell explained that the decision was one made out of practicality and concern for the safety of others.

Dellenbaugh went on to write two books: *Romance of the Colorado River* (1902), about the first expedition, and *A Canyon Voyage* (1908), about the second. Over the years, Dellenbaugh became Powell's greatest apologist.

In this vein, Dellenbaugh wrote: "Until the Major's unrivalled first descent in 1869 the river was equally unknown. Even about

Gunnison Crossing [near present-day Green River, Utah,], despite spasmodic efforts at exploration referred to, the river had remained a geographical enigma, and to the Major belongs the sole credit for solving this great problem throughout its length from the Union Pacific crossing in Wyoming to the mouth of the Virgin River—the last problem of this kind within the United States."

Dellenbaugh's description of Powell in *Romance of the Colorado River* is telling: "In these travels he [Powell] formed his plans for an attempt to fully explore, by means of a boat voyage, the remarkable string of chasms which for more than three centuries had defied examination. He decided that the starting point must be where the Union Pacific Railway had just been thrown across Green River, and that the only chance for success was to continue on the torrential flood till either he should arrive at the end of the great canyons near the mouth of the Rio Virgen or should himself be vanquished in the endeavor. It was to be a match of human skill and muscle against rocks and cataracts, shut in from the outer world, always face to face with the Shadow of Death. It was to be a duel to the finish between the mysterious torrent on the one side and a little group of valiant men on the other. Never had plumed knight of old a more dreadful antagonist."

Dellenbaugh continued: "Like the Sleeping Beauty, this strange Problem lay in the midst of an enchanted land guarded by the wizard Aridity and those wonderful water-gods Erosion and Corrasion, waiting for the knight-errant brave, who should break the spell and vanquish the demon in his lair. No ordinary man was equal to this difficult task, which demanded not alone courage of the highest order, but combined with this courage a master-mind and the strategic skill of a general. But there comes a time for everything. The moment for shattering this mystery had apparently arrived and the mortal who was to achieve this wonderful feat enters upon the scene with the quiet nerve and perfect confidence of a master. He realized the gravity of the proposition and therein rested his strength. He knew no ordinary boat could hope to live in the turmoil of waters that lashed themselves to fury among the rocks and against the towering and continuous cliffs; and he knew the party must be self-supporting in every sense of the term, depending on nothing but their own powers and what they could carry along."

Dellenbaugh concluded: "The universal dread of the Colorado and its gorges had by this time considerably augmented. The public imagination pictured the roaring flood ploughing its dismal channel through dark subterranean galleries where human life would not be worth a single drop of tossing spray; or leaping at a bound over precipices beside which the seething plunge of Niagara was but a toy. No one could deny these weird tales. No one knew. But Powell was fortified by Science, and he surmised that nowhere would he encounter any obstruction which his ingenuity could not surmount."

After Powell's second expedition, it was almost another 20 years before the river was explored again. In May 1889, an entrepreneur named Frank Brown wanted to build a railroad alongside the river from the town of Green River, Utah, and into the Grand Canyon to southern California, in order to bring coal from the state of Colorado to the growing cities on the West Coast. He hired Robert Brewster Stanton as chief engineer, but the survey was a total failure. Boats and supplies were promptly destroyed in Cataract Canyon, and the crew eventually collected themselves at Lees Ferry, Arizona, where Brown announced, quite amazingly, that they would continue down the Grand Canyon.

The expedition portaged nearby Badger Rapid and camped below. That night Brown slept fitfully, concerned about the rapids ahead. In the lead boat with Brown was Harry McDonald, and neither man was wearing a life jacket. They soon came to Soap Creek Rapid, which they portaged. Shortly thereafter, Brown's boat hit turbulent waters and capsized. McDonald was able to swim to shore, but Brown never surfaced. Only his notebook was recovered.

In spite of the catastrophe of losing the leader of the expedition, Stanton insisted that they continue on. Expedition member Peter Hansborough expressed feelings of intense anxiety and depression. Stanton tried to encourage him, but with no success. Also along on the trip were two African Americans, Henry Richards and George Gibson, who were devoted employees of the Stanton family. They were worried, and read the Bible together and discussed deep spiritual matters.

The next morning, Stanton and Franklin Nims, the trip photographer, decided to walk along the bank and take photographs of the action.

Stanton pushed the boat carrying Hansborough and Richards from shore, and in short order the boat was swept against the canyon wall, where it quietly overturned. Before the others could come to their rescue, both Hansborough and Richards disappeared into the foam and drowned.

At that point, the trip was abandoned, and the surviving crew found a side canyon in which to escape to the north rim. As they started to climb out of the chasm, they turned around and saw Brown's body float by.

Stanton was determined to complete the journey. He returned a few months later, but this time he was equipped with life jackets and better boats. On the second leg of the 1890 expedition, Stanton found Peter Hansborough's body. The group identified his skeleton by his boots, and they buried him nearby after carving his name in the rocks close to a point that is now called Point Hansborough.

Stanton remained obsessed with the Colorado River, and he spent the rest of his life writing a voluminous history about its early travelers. The book was published posthumously in 1932 under the title *Colorado River Controversies*.

After the ill-fated Brown–Stanton expedition, the river remained silent for years. Powell spent the remainder of his life in a long and distinguished career as a government bureaucrat. In 1881, he was appointed the director of the U.S. Geological Survey, a post he held until he resigned in 1894. He also served as the director of the Bureau of Ethnology at the Smithsonian Institution. The Major died on September 23, 1902, at the age of 68.

As an interesting aside, Powell was a friend of W. J. McGee, who was president of the National Geographic Society at the time. The two wagered that each had the larger brain. This was an era, it should be remembered, when it was thought that intelligence was relative to the size of one's brain. Powell died ten years earlier than McGee, but later autopsies revealed that, in the end, the Major had the larger brain.

The rest of the members of the expedition faded into quiet anonymity, and not even a photograph remains of Bradley or Dunn.

Walter Powell never recovered from his debilitating mental disorder, and he lived a life dependent on others. He died in an insane asylum in Washington, DC, in 1915 at the age of 72.

Jack Sumner, who was interviewed by Robert Brewster Stanton decades later, married a few years after the journey, went on to have three sons, and worked in a mining business until he died in Vernal, Utah, in 1907, at the age of 67.

George Bradley left for California after the expedition. He was injured in an accident that left him paralyzed, and he moved back to his hometown of Newbury, Massachusetts. He died in 1885, at the age of 50, from medical complications resulting from his accident. His greatest legacy was the diary he kept on the river.

Bill Hawkins, who years later gave several interviews about the expedition, eventually married and moved to Graham County in southern Arizona. He farmed and ran livestock until his death in 1919 at the age of 71.

Andy Hall was dramatically killed when ambushed by armed robbers while accompanying a Wells Fargo shipment of gold to Globe, Arizona. He died in 1882 at the age of 32.

Frank Goodman died in Vernal, Utah, in 1915, at the age of 71, apparently without any regrets about abandoning the expedition early on.

The members of the Colorado River Exploring Expedition of 1869 were gone within less than 50 years of their notorious river journey. As for the written materials that survived the expedition, the *Utah Historical Quarterly* issue devoted to the expedition states:

Powell's journal, covering the period July 2 to August 28, 1869, amounts to less than thirty pages of brief notes, in some cases mere enumerations or phrases. The original Sumner diary is lost, as is also the copy which Sumner made at Fort Yuma for Major Powell. A somewhat mutilated copy (of Sumner's copy transcribed at Fort Yuma), made many years after the time of the expedition, is preserved. The period covered extends from July 6 to August 31. It is written in a foreign handwriting that has been copied three or four times. The Bradley diary which is in two parts, May 21 to June 28 and June 29 to August 30, each being numbered independently (pages 1–12, pages 1–28), is therefore the only complete day-to-day record of the expedition from the day it left Green River until its termination near Callville.

In addition to the diaries by Powell, Sumner, and Bradley, there were several other significant records of the expedition, including letters that Major Powell wrote to the Chicago Tribune, dated May 24, June 2–6, 7, 18–20, and 23 and to friends dated June 29; Oramel Howland wrote to the Rocky Mountain News on June 19 and July 1, and Walt Powell to the Chicago Evening Journal on July 3.

Long after the expedition was over, Robert Brewster Stanton extensively investigated the details of the journey, particularly the departure of the Howland brothers and Dunn at the end, as well as the improbable claim of James White to be the first man to float through the Grand Canyon. Stanton approached Powell for further information but found him uncooperative.

By pure chance, Stanton met Jack Sumner on the Colorado in December 1889, and through Sumner, Stanton then came into contact with Bill Hawkins. Interviewed by Stanton, both Sumner and Hawkins—speaking independently—provided remarkably similar stories that cast serious doubts on the veracity of Powell's official report.

PART VI

AFTERMATH

★ ★ ★ ★

CHAPTER TWENTY-FOUR

WORKING AS A COMMERCIAL RAFTING GUIDE ON THE Colorado River in the Grand Canyon between summers of college (many years ago now, but with a gratitude I can never repay), I had the pleasure of delving deeply into my battered copy of Powell's justly celebrated work, *Exploration of the Colorado River and Its Canyons.*

Sitting around a roaring campfire in the depths of the canyon, the guides would read aloud from this marvelous tale. With the light of the flames flickering off the canyon walls, we reveled in Powell's stirring prose at night as we followed in his watery wake by day. It was high drama and, I must say, more than a little intoxicating.

The Major became a hero of mine, as he has been for many others privileged enough to ply the roiling waters of this magnificent river and its marvelous canyons. Not surprisingly, Powell is the subject of several glowing biographies by well-known historians, many of which have extolled him as an explorer on par with the likes of Columbus and Magellan. Donald Worster wrote of Powell in *A River Running West*: "He had ambition, scope, determination, and a willingness to risk all for the sake of science. Thereafter, the Colorado and its tributaries would rightfully be identified with him."

Powell achieved remarkable accomplishments in the exploration of the American West. He brought back vital topographical, geological, botanical, and other scientific knowledge of this unknown territory. He explored in detail the depths of one of the world's greatest natural wonders—the Grand Canyon—and the tremendous rapids and waterfalls in its imposing gorges. He became an influential spokesman for the environmental issues that would face this drought-ridden region as it became populated with westward expansion. He was a strong advocate for the indigenous people, befriending them and opening a channel of communication where there had been much misunderstanding.

In his book *The Emerald Mile*, Kevin Fedarko wrote, "Powell's presence is woven into the fabric of the canyon and haunts the river in ways that are impossible to ignore even today. His exploits are recounted and debated around each campfire, and a copy of his journal rides on almost every trip. On the maps that are used by the boatmen and guides, more than a hundred buttes, rapids, and plateaus bear the names that he and his men assigned to these features. He cut the line. He set the narrative. Everything that would subsequently unfold on the river . . . would flow from the themes that were inscribed by the one-armed major and his fleet of little wooden boats in the summer of 1869."

There is also no question that but for the persistence of Powell's initiative, the epic Colorado River Exploring Expedition of 1869 never would have occurred. Powell conceived of the expedition; sought to finance it largely with his own funds; ordered the boats; planned its myriad details; recruited its members; collected scientific data and specimens; made the hard decisions; and finally, saw the expedition through to its bitter end, succeeding when lesser men would have surely failed. Add to this his severe handicap—most of his right arm had been amputated after a gunshot wound at the Battle of Shiloh—in demanding physical circumstances, and you clearly have an individual of considerable initiative, courage, and fortitude.

But there is often another side to the story. After one scrutinizes the diaries and interviews of the other expedition members and looks closely at the actions of Powell himself, it is safe to say that Powell had significant limitations in his leadership and the way he treated his men. Many of those who look closely at the record have concluded that the expedition succeeded in reaching the Gulf of California not because of Powell, but in spite of him. This pronouncement may be a little harsh, but the case for criticism of Powell's judgment has sturdy foundations if one delves beyond the literary veneer.

First descents into inhospitable terrain are invariably difficult endeavors, and second-guessing the decisions of those who have ventured into such harrowing situations is rarely fair game, especially after decades have passed. But if the facts bear it out, an undeserved reputation shrouded in untouchable mystique should be exposed.

To analyze the situation, let's look briefly at the evidence. First of all, consider the wooden boats that Powell designed and had custom-built for the descent. Frederick Dellenbaugh, of the second Powell expedition, wrote that, "To anyone wishing to try the descent of the Colorado, I commend these boats as being perhaps as well as adapted to the work as any that can be devised."

In spite of Dellenbaugh's endorsement, the boats were undoubtedly better suited for rowing across the calm waters of Lake Michigan than dodging the perilous rapids of rock-infested rivers. Featuring low sides, rounded hulls, and pronounced keels, they were unwieldy and prone to tipping—hardly the characteristics one needs when negotiating tortuous whitewater.

While it is no doubt true that knowledge of fast-water boating was limited at that time, there was experience available. After all, Lewis and Clark had descended the formidable rapids of the Salmon River 60 years earlier, and there were many individuals who negotiated swift rivers while hunting, fishing, and trapping who could have been consulted on boat design.

Three of the four boats were made with double planks of cured oak, rendering them extraordinarily heavy. Powell must have known that many of the rapids were so menacing they would have to be portaged. With boats and supplies weighing thousands of pounds, the task of transporting this much weight presented a significant dilemma.

Powell anticipated that the journey might require wintering over, so he packed enough provisions for ten months. An undertaking this formidable required significant stores of food and clothing; guns, ammunition, and traps for hunting; and tools for building winter shelters. But the substantial weight of this load further slowed the party's progress downriver. In the end, the expedition took only a hundred days to complete, not ten months.

Far preferable would have been lighter craft and fewer provisions that allowed for a swifter and less complicated descent. The fourth boat, the one Powell traveled in, was constructed of pine and was far superior for handling and portaging. In other words, the albatross of behemoth boats nearly killed the party, and unnecessarily so. As the expedition's leader, much of the blame necessarily lies with Powell.

The boats were also poorly waterproofed, and the food inside quickly spoiled, further hastening the men's desperate need to escape the canyons to prevent dying of starvation. While equipment was less sophisticated than it is today, outdoorsmen had been working in climates far wetter and more inhospitable than those found here. Why Powell did not devote more thought and resources to protecting this lifeblood of the expedition is not readily apparent.

Powell was aware that the river was littered with whitewater, and he himself had gazed deep into some of its canyons. As a geologist, he knew that huge sheets of the rock face had fallen from the canyon walls to create rapids of enormous consequence. And yet Powell was the only member of the expedition who wore a life jacket, a fact he later took some lengths to conceal. With the loss of an arm, Powell certainly needed the additional flotation more than the able-bodied members, but these were some of the most dangerous cataracts on the face of the earth. The lack of life jackets might have been an austerity measure, but surely corners could have been cut elsewhere. On numerous occasions the men were precariously swept down the river, and it was a miracle that no one drowned.

Even the timing of the expedition's departure was in some ways ill conceived. The party pushed off in late May, which meant there was considerable snowmelt in the surrounding mountains. Powell had spent the previous two summers in the West, so he knew firsthand about runoff and its effect on rising river levels. In running rivers, high water is almost always dangerous water (especially when it is cold) because the margins of error are narrowed with the increased speed of the current. Tackling the river at any other time of year, when the flows were lower, would have made more sense. The oppressive heat of the desert in summer also quickly drained the strength and resolve of the men to continue in these arduous conditions.

Another costly error was the failure to distribute valuable gear among the four boats should one be lost. This was especially true of the scientific instruments, which were essential to determining the expedition's geographical location and progress downstream. When a boat was lost early in the journey, it was unfortunately the one that contained all of the barometers. Powell's failure to supervise such critical details should have been embarrassing. Instead, he chose to take his anger out on the men and blame them for the error.

The expedition was severely compromised when the *No Name* was lost. A few weeks later, the party was within striking distance of a trading post at the Indian reservation, but they brought back very little food. In their journals the men later grumbled about this critical decision, for which they suffered debilitating hunger pains.

Then there was the staffing of the expedition. None of the men had any significant experience around boats, but if Powell had diligently searched for such expertise, he could have found individuals familiar with moving water. Most of the men he selected were retired from the military, and they knew how to hunt and trap, but little else. Such skills may have been valuable in the mountains, but they were of limited use in the desert. Powell relied on supplementing the group's larder with wild game, but these were very sparse hunting grounds.

Powell's personnel decisions were sometimes hastily and impulsively made. He recruited the last two members of the expedition just as the group was about to depart. One of them deserted the venture a few weeks later. Another significant liability for the crew was Powell's brother, a sulky and brooding individual with a serious mental illness who would prove detrimental to the group's morale.

Even though Powell spoke of how fond he was of the men, their diaries reflected something different. Dunn was a devoted crew member—one who assumed risky positions on top of boulders as the men lined the unruly boats. On one occasion, Dunn became tangled in the ropes and almost drowned. Unbeknownst to Dunn, one of the Major's watches was still in Dunn's pocket as he fell into the water, and it was ruined.

When Powell discovered this loss, he harshly demanded that Dunn pay for the watch on the spot or hike out of the canyon immediately. In response, Bradley and the Howland brothers warned Powell that if Dunn were forced to leave, they would join him. The confrontation left a bitter taste in Dunn's mouth, and he abandoned the group in its last days.

A few days later, another violent confrontation between Dunn and Powell elicited this reaction from crew member Hawkins: "Sumner and I had all we could do to keep down mutiny. There was bad feeling from that time on for a few days. We began not to recognize any authority from the Major."

Sumner added: "Major Powell did not run the outfit in the same overbearing manner after that. At a portage or bad let-down he took his geological hammer and kept out of the way." And yet Powell's biographers have ignored these conflicts, and many others, to preserve the Major's mythical reputation.

There was the issue of the money that Powell owed, but never repaid, to the men. In his interview with Robert Brewster Stanton, Hawkins spoke about the unpaid debts. Powell promised to pay Hawkins $960 for horse-packing equipment and three horses and mules. Powell also promised to replace Hawkins's 36 traps. Powell also agreed to pay Hawkins $1.50 a day as a cook, and if the government would appropriate $12,000, he would receive $1,000. Hawkins was to be reimbursed for transportation back to Colorado after the expedition was complete.

After the trip, Powell said he would send Hawkins a government voucher for the traps, provisions, and animals Hawkins sold him. When Hawkins later saw the Major and asked him about it, the Major said he was still waiting on an appropriation from the government. Other than the $60 Hawkins was given at the mouth of the Virgin River, he never received anything from the Major.

Sumner was treated likewise, except the Major owed him several thousand dollars. In his interview with Stanton, Sumner said, "Major Powell paid me but $75 for my two years' work. I paid out of my pocket more than a thousand dollars to make the trip a success. I have seen it in print, too, that the Major spent great sums of his own money to help the expedition along. May I kindly ask when and to whom he paid it? But he has passed over the range, and the Bookkeeper is there."

Powell made a few other promises he failed to keep—for example, this one from Sumner's journal entry of August 13:

> *About fifteen miles below the Little Colorado the first bad rapid occurs, in what I wanted to name Coronado Canyon. Major Powell told me it should bear my name if he got through and ever had the opportunity to place it on the Government map. Well, he got through all right, but he forgot his vows and named it Grand Canyon.*

Even the idea for the expedition is the subject of some controversy. Powell writes in his report:

> *In the summer of 1867, with a small party of naturalists, students, and amateurs like myself, I visited the mountain region of Colorado Territory. While in Middle Park, I explored a lit-*

tle canyon, through which the Grand River runs, immediately below the watering-place, "Middle Park Hot Springs." Later in the fall I passed through Cedar Canyon, the gorge by which the Grand leaves the park. A result of the summer's study was to kindle a desire to explore the canyons of the Grand, Green, and Colorado Rivers, and the next summer I organized an expedition with the intention of penetrating still farther into that canyon country.

Sumner had a slightly different version of how the idea for the journey transpired:

I fired back at him the counter-proposition—the exploration of the Colorado River of the West, from the junction of the Green and Grand Rivers to the Gulf of California. He at first scouted the idea as foolhardy and impossible. I urged on him the importance of the work and what a big feather it would be in our hats if we succeeded. After several windy fights around the campfire, I finally outwinded him, and it was agreed that we should come out the following spring and we should make the attempt. I believe Major Powell states in his report that the exploration of the Colorado River had been in his mind for years. He mentioned nothing of the kind to me previous to our discussion of and agreement to do it, and the idea was certainly not his own.

Because of these criticisms, many of Powell's biographers have gone to great lengths to discredit Sumner and paint him as embittered. But does this sound like the words of a cynic? "He [Powell] was a man of many traits, good, bad, and indifferent. He was vastly overestimated as a man, as so many others have been. As a scholar and scientist he was worthy of all praise. His body has gone to the dust and his soul back to God who gave it. Let us cast a mantle of charity over his faults."

The record is replete with examples of events on the river that were not as portrayed in Powell's report. The reality was in fact far more complicated than previously presented.

CHAPTER TWENTY-FIVE

THE TRUTH ABOUT THE POWELL EXPEDITION CAN perhaps best be understood by looking at what happened afterward.

With what some might call something of a debacle—rather than a resounding success—behind him, Powell returned to Washington, DC, where he became an instant national celebrity. Although Congress had initially been skeptical about the expedition, they were now—like all good politicians riding a crest of public enthusiasm—eager to hear the details of the journey and to lend their hearty endorsement to the venture.

So they pressed Powell for a written report about his journey, and they inquired about the possibility of a second expedition to collect further information about these unexplored reaches of the American West. Representative James A. Garfield, chairman of the House Appropriations Committee, went so far as to tell a financially distressed Powell that government funds for further explorations would be forthcoming only if a formal account of the trip was prepared and distributed by the government press.

Driven largely by this financial incentive, Powell wrote a book titled *Exploration of the Colorado River of the West and its*

Tributaries, which was published by the Government Printing Office in 1875. As it turned out, Powell's report was no dry scientific tome, but an adventure narrative of personal proportions.

For decades, river runners have reveled in Powell's work and its stirring prose about what it was like to first see the magnificent depths of these imposing gorges. This powerful account of the scenery and the perils looming inside these deep chasms deserves a preeminent place among literature of the wild and untamed rivers in the American West.

Unfortunately, there is a small problem with Powell's book: it was based on a lie. The 1869 report was made to look like a transcription of a daily diary. One could almost see the Major busily scribbling away in his journal while perched on the riverbank. For example, his entry for June 5 read:

> *Now, as I write, the sun is going down and the shadows are setting in the canyon. The vermilion gleams and the rosy hues, the green and gray tints are changing to somber brown above, and black shadows below. Now 'tis a black portal to a region of gloom. And that is the gateway through which we enter our voyage of exploration tomorrow—and what shall we find?*

But the so-called "diary" was no such thing. Not only was it written in Powell's comfortable study years later, it contained a combination of events from both the 1869 trip and the subsequent trip made in 1871–72 (which, oddly enough, was never mentioned in Powell's published report) with a completely different crew of men. Many events that occurred in 1871 and 1872 were said to have occurred in 1869, even to the date and hour, along with events that involved individuals who were not even present on the first expedition.

As if that weren't enough, many details about the river were clearly exaggerated. To put it politely, Powell's book exercised a great deal of "literary license." And Powell's failure to mention that there was a second expedition was obviously a slight to the men who had risked their lives there.

Robert Brewster Stanton—among the first to replicate Powell's journey downriver when, 20 years later, in 1889, he surveyed the river for the Colorado Canyon and Pacific Railroad Company—remarked about Powell's official report: "He was making an official report to the Smithsonian Institution and to the Congress of the United States upon a great scientific exploration. One certainly would have the right to expect in it accuracy as to facts and occurrences of the journey and the correct dates when these occurred, as well as a proper regard for accuracy in statements relating to the physical condition of the canyon walls."

Stanton asked Sumner about the three men who left the expedition in the river's lower reaches. When Stanton mentioned Powell's published description of the last rapid, Sumner responded bitterly, "There's lots in that book besides the truth!"

And with that bit of information, Stanton met Powell at his office in Washington, DC, in May 1892, 23 years after the expedition, and confronted him about the report. Powell looked Stanton straight in the eye and said that his report was in fact "his diary written on the spot."

The evidence, unfortunately, suggests strongly to the contrary. Consider, for a moment, Powell's diary entry for August 26. It states: "Found Indian camp today—gardens. Good run of 35 miles. Camp 42."

Contrast that brief statement with Powell's published report for the same day:

Since we left the Colorado Chiquito, we have seen no evidence of the tribe of Indians inhabiting the plateaus on either side ever come down to the river, but about eleven o'clock today we discover an Indian garden, at the foot of the wall on the right, just where a little stream, with a narrow flood-plain, comes down through a side canyon. Along the valley, the Indians have planted corn, using the water which burst out in springs at the foot of the cliff, for irrigation. The corn is looking quite well, but is not sufficiently advanced to give us roasting ears; but there are some nice, green squashes. We carry ten or a dozen of these on board our boats, and hurriedly leave, not willing to be caught in the robbery, yet excusing ourselves by pleading our great want. We run down a short distance, to where we feel certain no Indians can follow; and what a kettle of squash we make! True, we have no salt with which to season it, but it makes a fine addition to our unleavened bread and coffee. Never was fruit so sweet as those stolen squashes.

After dinner we push on again, making fine time, finding many rapids, but none so bad that we cannot run them with safety, and when we stop, just at dusk, and foot up our reckoning, we find we have run thirty-five miles again.

What a supper we make; unleavened bread, green squash sauce, and strong coffee. We have been for a few days on half rations, but we have no stint of roast squash. A few days like this we are out of prison.

This elaboration, one must admit, is quite an "embellishment" on the sketchy diary entry.

Or consider Powell's diary entry for August 17: "Make run of 10¼ miles today, with 2 bad portages. Camp at night just above one. Walk up creek 3 miles. Grand scenery. Old Indian camps.

Through this Canyon the limestone overlies the granite and ruins down near the river in sharp wall-like points. To the summit of this the largest rocks that can be seen at any point. I estimate the height at 4000 ft. may be only 3500. Camp No. 33."

Here is Powell's published report for the same day:

Our rations are still spoiling; the bacon is so badly injured that we are compelled to throw it away. By an accident, this morning, the saleratus [baking soda] is lost overboard. We have now only musty flour sufficient for ten days, a few dried apples, but plenty of coffee. We must make all haste possible. If we meet with difficulties, as we have done in the canyon above, we may be compelled to give up the expedition, and try to reach the Mormon settlements to the north. Our hopes are that the worst places are passed, but our barometers are all so much injured as to be useless, so we have lost our reckoning in altitude, and know not how much descent the river has yet to make.

The stream is still wild and rapid, and rolls through a narrow channel. We make but slow progress, often landing against a wall, and climbing around some point, where we can see the river below. Although very anxious to advance, we are determined to run with great caution, lest, by another accident, we lose all our supplies. How precious that little flour has become! We divide it among the boats, and carefully store it away, so that it can be lost only by the loss of the boat itself.

We make ten miles and a half, and camp among the rocks, on the right. We have had rain, from time to time, all day, and have been thoroughly drenched and chilled; but between showers the sun shines with great power, and the mercury in our thermometers stands at 115°, so that we have rapid changes from great extremes, which are very disagreeable. It is espe-

cially cold in the rain tonight. The little canvas we have is rotten and useless; the rubber ponchos, with which we started from Green River City, have all been lost; more than half the party is without hats, and not one of us has an entire suit of clothes, and we have not a blanket apiece. So we gather drift wood, and build a fire; but after supper the rain, coming down in torrents, extinguishes it, and we sit up all night, on the rocks, shivering, and are more exhausted by the night's discomfort than by the day's toil.

Perhaps even more disturbing is Powell's journal report for August 29, a sentimental description of what happened at Separation Rapid and the fate of the three men:

The river rolls by us in silent majesty; the quiet of the camp is sweet; our joy almost ecstasy. We sit till long after midnight talking of the Grand Canyon, talking of home, but talking chiefly of the three men who left us. Are they wandering in those depths, unable to find a way out? Are they searching over the desert lands above for water? Or are they nearing the settlements?

It is a macabre scene because we now know that Powell wrote this entry in his study at home years later when he knew full well that the Howland brothers and Dunn lay dead in the desert.

It is well established, then, that Powell's published report was not a diary penned on the spot. That fabrication could have been easily forgiven were it not for Powell's vehement insistence that it was.

Powell, it seems, was guilty of embellishing the facts, and he often doubled (or more) the severity of the rapids. For example, Powell's diary entry for July 24 is: "river fell by estimate 42 feet." Powell's official report for the day is: "[river had a] fall of 75 feet."

Another example is Powell's diary entry for August 14, which read: "[Sockdolager rapids has a] fall of 30 feet." Powell's report for the same day: "[Sockdolager rapids has a] descent of perhaps 75 or 80 feet."

A few other things struck Stanton after his personal encounter with Powell. After Stanton mentioned that he had recently spoken to his head boatmen, Jack Sumner, Powell seemed unaware that Sumner was still alive. Powell then became strangely defensive and attempted to belittle Stanton's journey by saying, "I went through without knowing what was before me. You knew all about it beforehand, and had a map."

The next year, in 1893—some 24 years after the expedition—Powell delivered an address about the expedition to the Irrigation Congress. Unbeknownst to Powell, Stanton was in the audience. Powell stated that since his trip no one had passed through the canyons—not only denying Stanton's trip four years earlier, but Powell's second journey in 1871. After the speech, Stanton pushed his way to the front of the crowd, shook Powell's hand, and said, "I simply want to let you know, Major, that I was in the audience and heard you."

An incensed Stanton, armed with all the confirmation he needed that Powell had lied, began to investigate all the claims in Powell's report and to interview as many members of the first expedition as he could. His scathing critique, titled *Colorado River Controversies*, was posthumously published in 1932 (and dedicated to "All Truthful Colorado River Voyageurs").

In his analysis, Stanton maintained that the Major's report was "in many instances distorted and exaggerated . . . demonstrably inaccurate, and it would seem, deliberately misleading on a number of counts . . . [revealing] that the Major was undoubtedly guilty of suppression of the truth and unblushing exaggeration."

The epic historical undertaking known as the Colorado River Exploring Expedition of 1869 is unique in that much of what happened in those lonely chasms in the earth can now be verified through diaries, interviews, and numerous writings of the men who participated in this momentous journey.

In an extremely fortuitous set of circumstances, Major Powell's former secretary came across his original handwritten notes in the corner of his office after he died, and she delivered them to Stanton. Stanton explained the remarkable discovery:

> *By this time the patience and interest of the whole office force— and I confess my persistency and hopes—were fast fading away. Then Miss Clark remarked: "By the way, over there in the corner under that old desk, which has not been used for years, are two or three bundles of old papers. I haven't the least idea what they contain, but if you wish to, you may look them over."*
>
> *The dust and cobwebs of years did not stop me. I took off my coat, rolled up my sleeves, and got to work with a feather duster. I opened the bundles and spread out their contents on the floor of Major Powell's old office. Almost the first thing I laid my eyes upon was the long-lost, long-sought-for Journal of the Exploration of 1869, in Major Powell's own hand writing—the original itself!*

From a comparison of the diary entries against the published report, it is obvious that Powell blended events from the two trips. When Powell later took his story about the 1869 expedition to the public, he refused to acknowledge there even was a second expedition.

Stanton had the presence of mind to interview several members of the expedition before they died and to collect their diaries before they were lost forever. These interviews and diaries make for fascinating reading and are greatly at odds with Powell's rosy portrayal of the journey.

Powell, for instance, never mentioned the acrimony that occurred early in the trip after the loss of the *No Name* at Disaster Falls, or the explosive situation that arose a month later when the Major's valuable watch was accidently damaged by William Dunn during a risky portage. It is clear that these events, and many others, led to the disastrous desertion—and subsequent death—of three men shortly before journey's end.

When *Colorado River Controversies* was published, 57 years had elapsed before a countervailing view about the expedition was entertained. Then, 15 years after that, in 1947, the *Utah Historical Quarterly*, in a thick volume containing a copious amount of information about the expedition, published the heretofore unseen diaries of all those who prepared them—Powell, Sumner, and Bradley—and the published articles of Major Powell, Walter Powell, and Oramel Howland.

In other words, 72 years had passed before the unvarnished diaries of Sumner and Bradley were revealed to the public. Until the publication of the *Utah Historical Quarterly*, the Powell version was taken as gospel. Its editor, William Culp Darrah, stated: "When [Frederick S.] Dellenbaugh [a member of the second Powell expedition] prepared his account of the first expedition he knew only of the Major's incomplete diary and a few notes from an incomplete and brief journal on foolscap kept by Jack Sumner on the first trip. Dellenbaugh wrote that he did not believe that any other member of the 1869 expedition had kept a journal of the events. This erroneous opinion has been repeated by every other written on the canyon down to the present time [1947]."

Perhaps more interesting than Powell's refusal to acknowledge the fabrications in his published report and the existence of a second expedition is the willingness of a cadre of professional and well-respected historians to turn a blind eye to anything even remotely critical of Major Powell.

The foremost Powell biography, a thick tome titled *Beyond the Hundredth Meridian*, was published by the renowned historian Wallace Stegner in 1954—79 years after the publication of Powell's report and 85 years after the expedition. Powell died in 1902, and the other members of the expedition had been deceased for many decades, so Stegner was obviously working from second-hand sources.

Stegner did, however, have access to Stanton's work and to the *Utah Historical Quarterly*, which discussed these contentions. Amazingly enough, Stegner's exhaustive work is silent about the substantial liberties that Powell took with the truth as he compiled his account of one of the West's most important explorations.

In his book, *Colorado River Country*, the prolific Western historian David Lavender summed up the situation: "The flaws in the *Exploration* account are Powell's invention of exciting episodes for dramatic relief; his use, as though they had happened in 1869, of events and place names taken from the 1871–72 run down the river without so much as a mention of the second venture or its personnel . . ." This, it seems to me, is a fair and objective commentary.

In the introduction to his official journal, Powell declared (we now know, disingenuously) that the report was in fact his diary: "I decided to publish this journal, with only such emendations and corrections as its hasty writing in camp necessitated." Interestingly,

Powell's diary consisted of about 3,000 words, but his published journal contained 100,000.

There have been a few individuals who have confronted some of the less-than-flattering facts about Powell. For example, William Culp Darrah—who held Powell in high regard and published a glowing biography about him in 1951—conceded that Powell's report was in essence a work of fiction. Darrah noted in his book, *Powell of the Colorado*, that, "The account given by the Major is a literary composition rather than a scientific document," and "The Major was not blameless when it comes to deliberate inaccuracy."

But staunch supporters of Powell would have none of it. Even when confronted with overwhelming evidence of the Major's transgressions, they quickly came to his rescue. Their rationalizations for the Major's "misstatements" often verge on the ludicrous. For example, Lewis R. Freeman, in his 1923 book, *The Colorado River: Yesterday, Today and Tomorrow*, admitted that Powell's report might have been a fraud, but explained that the report's "slight anachronisms" were committed "unwittingly."

It is difficult to imagine a man of Powell's intelligence was not completely aware of what he was doing. Freeman explains the "discrepancy" this way: "The narrative portion of Powell's report is in the form of a journal, with the incidents of each day entered in sequence. This is not the rough diary kept on the voyage, however, but a considerably polished expansion of it, probably written at least three years subsequently. This is proven by the fact that the author, doubtless writing in unrecorded occurrences from memory, unwittingly incorporated in his report of the initial voyage incidents which befell in the later one of 1872. These slight anachronisms, as Mr. Dellenbaugh has stated in calling one of them to my attention, are of negligible importance. The narrative itself—with its admirably maintained balance of informative detail, dramatic incident and humorous anecdote—is as much a classic as a story of scientific adventure, as the voyage which inspired it is a classic of exploration."

W. L. Rusho, in his 1969 book, *Powell's Canyon Voyage*, reasoned likewise. Powell fabricated the truth, according to Rusho, because "good storytelling" demanded it. Rusho also argued that Powell always considered the two trips to be just "one" exploration. It is logical to ask why, if it was just one exploration, the names of the other nine men were never mentioned.

Rusho argued that those who pointed out the truth were troublemakers: "Detractors point out that Powell sometimes altered the actual history of the 1869 expedition by combining with it events that did not happen until the second expedition, or by changing the sequence of events. But such changes are minor to one who reads the report as a tale of adventure. Powell thought of the two trips as one exploration in two parts. Omission of the names of the personnel of the second expedition was perhaps justified by the dictates of good storytelling."

One wonders what the hardworking members of the second expedition—who for little or no remuneration risked their lives in the endeavor—would have thought about being omitted from the report for the sake of a good narrative line.

The Powell apologists are quick to discredit anyone who speaks out against the Major. Jack Sumner later gave a detailed interview that was critical of Powell. In his biography, *Powell of the Colorado*, William Culp Darrah passes this off as mere bitterness, which he says must be discounted. According to Darrah, Sumner was the one with the problem, not Powell.

Note in particular Darrah's terse ad hominem attacks against Sumner: "With the years Sumner in particular had grown bitter, and as misfortunes heaped upon him, the bitter increased," and

"Sumner in later years became embittered against Powell. The statements attributed to Jack Sumner from 1890 to 1907 must be interpreted in this light." It also should be noted that Powell owed Sumner money that he never repaid.

Darrah likewise attacked Robert Brewster Stanton's extensive and well-documented critique as "hypercritical of Powell," writing that "the facts are manhandled in a reprehensible manner." Darrah fails to elaborate exactly how Stanton distorted the facts.

Author Lewis R. Freeman, once again, came to the defense of the Major, explaining why the frictions among the crew were never discussed by Powell: "That the explorer did not put on record the personal dissensions that were rife in his party was due to two reasons: one, because things of that kind had no place in a government report, and the other, because he was too big a man to let the memory of petty passages due to irritations of the voyage obscure his appreciation of the fact that it was to the devotion and courage of his men that he owed the triumphant outcome of the trip."

Frederick S. Dellenbaugh, a member of Powell's second expedition, went on to explain the situation in his book, *Romance of the Colorado River* (not published until 1902, more than 30 years after the second expedition), as an omission consciously committed for the sake of "dramatic unity": "When his report to Congress was published, Major Powell, perhaps for the sake of dramatic unity, concluded to omit mention of the personnel of the second expedition, awarding credit, for all that was accomplished, to the men of his first wonderful voyage of 1869. And these men surely deserved all that could be bestowed on them. They had, under the Major's clear-sighted guidance and cool judgment, performed one of the distinguished feats of history. They had faced unknown dangers. They had determined that the forbidding torrent could be mastered. But it has always seemed to me that the men of the second party, who made the same journey, who mapped and explored the river and much of the country roundabout, doing a large amount of difficult work in the scientific line, should have been accorded some recognition."

Clearly hurt by the omission, Dellenbaugh, in his second book, *A Canyon Voyage* (1908), wrote about his discussion with Powell concerning the issue, which clearly continued to bother him: "The absence of this has sometimes been embarrassing for the reason that when statements of members of the second party were referred to the official report, their names were found missing from the list. This inclined to produce an unfavorable impression concerning these individuals. In order to provide in my own case against any unpleasant circumstance owing to this omission, I wrote to Major Powell on the subject and received (to him anyway) the following highly satisfactory answer:

Washington, DC
January 18, 1888.
My Dear Dellenbaugh:

Replying to your note of the 14th instant, it gives me great pleasure to state that you were a member of my second party of exploration down the Colorado, during the years 1871 and 1872, that you occupied a place in my own boat and rendered valuable services to the expedition, and that it was with regret on my part that your connection with the Survey ceased.

Yours cordially,
J. W. Powell

Dellenbaugh, one of Powell's most ardent apologists, may have been "highly satisfied" with the evasive response he received from Powell, but surely not everyone on the second expedition was so easily consoled.

Almon Thompson, Powell's brother-in-law and a member of the 1871–72 expedition, was one of those not so easily appeased. He later wrote Dellenbaugh: "The phase of the Major's character which led him to ignore the second expedition is no mystery to me. He had no fine sense of justice, no exacted loyalty to a high ideal and honor and so far as his subordinates concerned did not know the meaning of noblesse oblige. He was generous, sympathetic, and possessed all the estimable qualities you and I assign him but you will notice neither you nor I speak of his justice or loyalty. He was sadly deficient in these."

Even present-day historian Donald Worster came to Powell's defense in his biography, *A River Running West* (published in 2000): "An arrogant pup like Stanton challenging an aging man's memory of his past glories should have expected to get that cold shoulder." Worster also argued that Powell treated Stanton rudely because of the tense political situation in Washington, DC, concerning Powell's bureaucratic role as the head of an irrigation survey. Worster explained: "Another hot, muggy summer lay ahead, another encounter with Senator Stewart [over matters related to reclamation in the West], and if the Major seemed nervous and defensive, then so was the whole city in a nervous mood, with tempers running high and unease creeping from one chamber to another."

One must also ask: why, if Powell was so fond of his colleagues, did he never inquire about them after the journey?

As for Thompson's criticism of Powell, Worster said: "This has the familiar, grudging tone of a brother-in-law who always resented the relative who had outshone him in every way. As for loyalty, Powell rescued Thompson from a small-town school superintendent's job, gave him a priceless opportunity to spend years in the West's most stunning and unspoiled region, and then maneuvered him into a well-paid, high-level career in the scientific establishment in Washington."

In the end, the Colorado River Exploring Expedition contained more than its share of difficult and uncertain moments. When the crew was starving to death in the heat of the desert and emotions among them had become raw-edged, they must have thought the next day would never come. Searching for the truth about what really happened so long ago in the depths of those desolate chasms seems a reasonable testament to the brave men who served the expedition, especially with so many historians stretching credulity to justify the behavior of Major Powell.

CHAPTER TWENTY-SIX

AFTER ALL THESE YEARS, THE UNANSWERED QUES-
tion of the Powell expedition remains: Why did Oramel Howland,
Seneca Howland, and Bill Dunn leave the expedition only two
days short of its termination?

Responding to that question, William Culp Darrah wrote:
"No more bitter controversy reflects upon Powell's leadership of
the expedition than the affair at Separation Rapids. Yet the simple
fact is they were afraid to go farther and deserted—with consent,
however; they were free to go."

Expedition member Andy Hall, in a letter to his brother a
month after the expedition, minced no words: "Adding further
to the conundrum, three diaries were compiled at the time of the
expedition—Powell's, Bradley's, and Sumner's—and none of them
mentions the unpleasant circumstances that might have led the
three men to leave the group in the waning moments of the journey downstream. Later interviews and statements of Sumner and
Hawkins, taken independently of each other, were consistent with
one another and were replete with criticisms of the Major."

The *Utah Historical Quarterly* issue devoted to the expedition, considered the most definitive collection of materials available, points out the controversy that remains unsolved to this day: "Thus, the scattered and fragmentary nature of the documented history of the exploration has left several puzzling questions which have never been answered. The most serious of these is the reason for the defection of the three men who deserted within hours of deliverance from the harrowing experience of the trip."

The initial inquiry is *how* the decision was made for the three men to leave and *who* initiated that action. Let's first look at the fairly lengthy entry for August 27 in Powell's report, which states that it was the Howland brothers and Dunn who decided to leave the group and that Powell was steadfast in his resolution to continue on. The Major clearly implied in his journal entry that the men leaving the expedition were doing so because they were afraid of the rapids ahead:

After supper Captain Howland asks to have a talk with me. We walk up the little creek a short distance, and I soon find that his object is to remonstrate against my determination to proceed. He thinks that we had better abandon the river here. Talking with him, I learn that he, his brother, and William Dunn have determined to go no farther in the boats. So we return to camp. Nothing is said to the other men.

For the last two days our course has not been plotted. I sit down and do this now, for the purpose of finding where we are by dead reckoning. It is a clear night, and I take out the sextant to make observation for latitude, and I find that the astronomic determination agrees very nearly with that of the plot—quite as closely as might be expected from a meridian observation on a planet. In a direct line, we must be about 45 miles from the mouth of the Rio Virgen. If we can reach that point, we know that there are settlements up that river about 20 miles. This 45 miles in a direct line will probably be 80 or 90 by the meandering line of the river. But then we know that there is comparatively open country for many miles above the mouth of the Virgen, which is our point of destination.

As soon as I determine all this, I spread my plot on the sand and wake Howland, who is sleeping down by the river, and show him where I suppose we are, and where several Mormon settlements are situated.

We have another short talk about the morrow, and he lies down again; but for me there is no sleep. All night long I pace up and down a little path, on a few yards of sand beach, along by the river. Is it wise to go on? I go to the boats again to look at our rations. I feel satisfied that we can get over the danger immediately before us; what there may be below I know not. From our outlook yesterday on the cliffs, the canyon seemed to make another great bend to the south, and this, from our experience heretofore, means more and higher granite walls. I am not sure that we can climb out of the canyon here, and, if at the top of the wall, I know enough of the country to be certain that it is a desert of rock and sand between this and the nearest Mormon town, which, on the most direct line, must be 75 miles away. True, the late rains have been favorable to us, should we go out, for the probabilities are that we shall find water still standing in holes; and at one time I almost conclude to leave the river. But for years I have been contemplating this trip. To leave the exploration unfinished, to say that there is a part of the canyon which I cannot explore, having already nearly accomplished it, is more than I am willing to acknowledge, and I determine to go on.

I wake my brother and tell him of Howland's determina-

tion, and he promises to stay with me; then I call up Hawkins,
the cook, and he makes a like promise; then Sumner and Brad-
ley and Hall, and they all agree to go on.

Bill Hawkins, however, offers a completely different view. Hawkins's version, as related in *Colorado River Controversies*, indicates
that Powell had decided to abandon the expedition until Hawkins
suggested they forge onward:

The Major, the Howland brothers, Dunn, and Sumner went
off to one side to hold another council. Bradley came over to
where Andy Hall and I were standing and completely broke
down and shed tears, and said such actions made him feel like
a child again. By that time the Major came up to where we
were standing and said, "Well, Billy, we have concluded to
abandon the river for the present," stating that on account of
the scarcity of provisions and because the rapids were getting
more severe, he thought the better thing to do was to leave the
river, as it could not be more than one hundred miles to some
settlement in Utah, and that we would get a new supply of grub
and return and complete our journey. By that time all the boys
were standing and listening to him. When he finished his say,
I asked him if he would sell the boat to Andy and me. He said
if we would come back and finish the trip he would give us the
boat. I told him I proposed to finish my part of it then.

I said, "Major, you have always looked to Hall and me as
being too young to have anything to say in your council, but
Hall and I are going to go down this river whether you or any of
the rest go or not." And I told him that if he left the river I would
not think of following him one foot on land, that my mind was
set. Then the Major said, "Well, Billy, if I have one man that

will stay with me I will continue my journey or be drowned in the attempt." I told him that Bradley, Hall, and I had made up our minds to continue and that I thought the worst of the rapids were passed, and that if he had taken me into his council he would have soon found out my attitude on that point.

Sumner spoke up and said, "Stay with it, Billy, and I will be with you." It did not take long to settle the rest of it. The Howland brothers and Dunn had made up their minds and would not change them. Of course, we knew what was the reason Dunn left. As for any fear, he did not possess it. And as for the other boys, they never showed any signs of fear. The elder of the Howlands had been in the boat with me since his own boat was wrecked.

As for the allegation that Powell ordered the three men to leave the expedition, the various diaries of the men (and even the later interviews of Sumner and Hawkins) show no evidence of such instructions. The split among the men appears to have been amiable, with each side trying to convince the other. This is not to say there was not acrimony between the Howlands and Dunn and the Major. The trouble between the Howlands and Powell extended back to Disaster Falls, and the ill feeling between Dunn and Powell arose in Cataract Canyon when Dunn lost the Major's watch.

Bradley's detailed diary shows no indication that the men were forced out. He wrote on August 27: "There is discontent in camp tonight and I fear some of the party will take to the mountains but hope not." Bradley's entry of August 28 clearly states that there is no ill feeling among the men:

Three men refused to go farther (two Howlands and Wm Dunn) and we had to let them take to the mountains. They left

*us with good feelings though we deeply regret their loss for they
are as fine fellows as I ever had the good fortune to meet.*

Likewise, Sumner's diary contains no evidence of an ouster.
Sumner writes in his diary on August 28:

*O. G. Howland and W. H. Dunn decided to abandon the out-
fit and try to reach the settlements on the head of the Virgin
River. Each took a gun and all the ammunition he wanted and
some provisions and left us to go it or swamp.*

Regardless of all this, Hawkins still felt the Major had dispar-
aged the reputations of the three men who left the expedition. In
his interview with Stanton, Hawkins said:

*I can say one thing truthfully about the Major—that no man
living was ever thought more of by his men up to the time he
wanted to drive Dunn from the party. . . . I have only written
here a few facts on things that happened on the Colorado expedition. There is no revenge in my heart. With the best of feelings
toward the Major, I have written this because I think his Report
is somewhat lacking. I am willing to do more by him than he
ever did any of us men. I am willing to call him a brave and
daring leader, but I do not think the boys who left the party,
the Howland brothers and Bill Dunn, under the circumstances
herein mentioned, deserve to be branded as cowards.*

Hawkins then continued with his criticism of Powell:

*I do not wish to cast any discredit on Major Powell's Report or
upon his memory of the Colorado expedition. But in justice to*

*Dunn and the Howland brothers I must say that the account in
the Report which accuses them of cowardice is entirely wrong,
and that it was made to cover up the real cause of their leaving.*

The controversy over the episode at Separation Rapids reached
an apex years later when Congress constructed a bronze memorial to the expedition on the south rim of the Grand Canyon. It
included the names of the five members of the 1869 expedition
that accompanied Powell, as well as the names of the six individuals on the 1871–72 expedition. It did *not* include the names of
Dunn and the Howland brothers.

The inscription on the Powell monument erected by Congress reads:

1869	1872
JOHN C SUMNER	A H THOMPSON
WALTER H POWELL	F S DELLENBAUGH
G Y BRADLEY	JOHN K HILLERS
WILLIAM R HAWKINS	STEPHEN V JONES
ANDREW HALL	W CLEMENT POWELL
	ANDREW J HATTAN

ERECTED BY THE CONGRESS OF THE UNITED STATES
TO MAJOR JOHN WESLEY POWELL FIRST EXPLORER OF
THE GRAND CANYON WHO DESCENDED THE RIVER
WITH HIS PARTY IN ROW-BOATS TRAVERSING THE
GORGE BENEATH THIS POINT AUGUST 17 1869 AND
AGAIN SEPTEMBER 1 1872

Writing in the *Utah Historical Quarterly* issue, William Culp
Darrah elaborated on the monument controversy and the insult,

intentional or not, to the three men who had spent 97 of the 99 days on the first expedition: "A more sentimental reason for weighing the evidence in this case is that the names of the Howland brothers and William Dunn were not placed on the memorial which now stands on the brink of the Grand Canyon as a tribute to the intrepid men who first explored the Grand Canyon of the Colorado. They deserved, perhaps, as much credit as the six members of the 1871–1872 party whose names are given on the tablet, yet who had abandoned the river before completing a passage; thus it was an appropriate honor paid them when Julius Stone and Dr. Russell G. Frazier, on August 28, 1939, affixed to the canyon wall at the point where they separated from Powell, a bronze plaque in their memory."

The plaque at Separation Rapids reads:

HERE ON AUGUST 28
1869
SENECA HOWLAND, O. G. HOWLAND,
AND
WILLIAM H. DUNN

SEPARATED FROM THE ORIGINAL
POWELL PARTY, CLIMBED TO
THE NORTH RIM AND WERE
KILLED BY THE INDIANS.

FOR FURTHER AUTHENTIC
INFORMATION SEE "COLORADO
RIVER CONTROVERSIES"
OBTAINABLE FROM UNIVERSITY LIBRARIES.

THIS CENOTAPH WAS PLACED
AND DEDICATED IN 1939 BY LATER COLORADO
RIVER VOYAGERS

In his introduction to *A Canyon Voyage*, Frederick Dellenbaugh defended the omission of the men's names on the Powell monument: "There has been some adverse criticism of the omission but it seems very clear that three men who refused to finish the journey and hampered the progress and success of the undertaking by backing out at a critical moment deserve no honorable mention."

Perhaps Donald Worster, in his biography *A River Running West*, summed it up best: "And the fate of the men who had determined to walk out of the canyon? Tellingly, Powell did not organize a search party to go look for them. It would be another year, in fact, before he made any effort to track them down, and then it would be done as part of a more general survey of Indians and geography north of the canyon. The men had left of their own will, rejecting entreaties and his leadership. They had used the rapids as an excuse more than as a reason to leave, or they would have followed after when they saw the party go through unscathed. Bad feelings, not rough water, was the real cause of their separation, a fact that Powell understood all too well. Although publicly he would say nothing harsh against them, he was manifestly not torn with anguish about their fate."

The issue of why Oramel Howland, Seneca Howland, and Bill Dunn left the venture so close to its end will continue to be debated by boaters around flickering campfires not far from where the three men stepped away from the expedition and walked into the vast wilderness beyond.

EPILOGUE

A CENTURY AND A HALF AFTER THE POWELL EXPEDI-
tion pulled their boats out of the water at Grand Wash Cliffs, it is
interesting to speculate how the brave explorers would react to the
scene now. Many changes have occurred to the river and the chasms
those men so desperately struggled through, not to mention the
hordes of individuals who have followed in their perilous path.

Perhaps the most dramatic change in the landscape is the massive reservoirs that now inundate large stretches of the river—
Flaming Gorge Reservoir, Lake Powell, and Lake Mead—making
a reenactment of the 1869 journey physically impossible.

The sport of river running has now become something of a
national pastime, and the number of those who participate in the
endeavor is astounding. The demand to traverse what is left of the
Green and Colorado Rivers is so intense that the federal agencies
that manage those rivers have instituted an allocation system with
the issuance of permits determined by lottery. These restrictions
are imperative because of the limited number of campsites in these
deep chasms, as well as the need to maintain at least the semblance
of wilderness.

But this is a wilderness no more. A typical summer day will see scores of boaters crowded around the boat launch, and the competition for choice campsites downstream can be intense. On many stretches of the river, massive, motorized, 37-foot pontoon boats run by commercial companies take a dozen or so passengers and all their gear downriver, often serving their clients gourmet food prepared by urban chefs (excursions known as the "float and bloat"), entertaining them with small symphonies, or educating them with lectures by professional geologists or historians.

Noncommercial boaters log into their computers and choose dates, keep their fingers crossed, and pray that the lottery will be good to them. The odds of drawing a permit for the Grand Canyon and the Gates of Lodore are especially daunting, although permits for Cataract and Desolation Canyons are not assured either. The Grand Canyon used to have a waiting list that accumulated from year to year, but when the wait reached 20 years, the National Park Service was forced to implement the lottery system. Some boaters have applied to secure a spot for decades without success, and many will inevitably die or become enfeebled before drawing a permit.

The hardier souls are accepting spots in January and February. With improved dry suits and other equipment, the trip is more comfortable than it used to be, but the cold water and limited sunlight still make this an endeavor only for the very robust. Chat rooms on the Internet make it possible for boaters to exchange thoughts about the latest gear, lodge complaints against the federal agencies managing the river resource, and even beg for spots on trips secured by fellow boaters.

The craft for such trips has clearly improved. The large inflatable raft with self-bailing floors has made it easier and safer to brave the rapids, which have not lessened in severity since Powell encountered them. A range of rowing frames, waterproof bags and boxes, and state-of-the-art coolers, stoves, and kitchen appliances have made it possible to eat fresh and expensive food for weeks on end.

The appeal of such legendary river trips has not lessened with time. Kevin Fedarko, in his book *The Emerald Mile*, speaks of the canyon in reverential terms that any canyon aficionado can relate to: "On any given evening in summer, but most notably in late June, there comes a moment just after the sun has disappeared behind the rimrock. . . . This is also the canyon's loveliest hour, when there is nothing sweeter, nothing more calming to the soul, than standing alone in the shallows at the edge of the Colorado River and breathing in the wonder of the place. The ramparts rising nakedly for more than a vertical mile above. The locomotive slabs that have peeled away from the terraced cliffs and shattered to pieces far below. And most bewitching of all, the muscular, sluicing, glimmer-gilded surface of the great river itself."

The challenges of the river have not changed much with time either. More than a hundred years ago, Frederick Dellenbaugh expressed it well: "Indeed, each person who first looks into the abyss has a sensation of being a discoverer, for the scene is so weird and lonely and so incomprehensible in its novelty that one feels that it could never have been viewed before. And it is rather a discovery for each individual, because no amount of verbal or pictorial description can ever fully prepare the spectator for the sublime reality."

Major Powell and his intrepid crew will always have the distinction of being the first to run through the forbidden abyss. But thankfully, there are those of us—the ones fortunate enough to follow in the footsteps of their wild and daunting journey—who remain explorers in our own right as we plunge into the depths of these glorious chasms.

APPENDIX 1

Powell on Geography and Geology

In his 1895 book, *Canyons of the Colorado*, Major Powell revised his original report of 1875 and included two interesting discussions of the geography of the Green and Colorado Rivers and the geology of the Grand Canyon, portions of which are reprinted here:

THE VALLEY OF THE COLORADO

The Colorado River is formed by the junction of the Grand and Green. The Grand River [now the headwaters of the Colorado River] has its source in the Rocky Mountains, five or six miles west of Long's Peak. A group of little alpine lakes, that receive their waters directly from perpetual snowbanks, discharge into a common reservoir known as Grand Lake, a beautiful sheet of water. Its quiet surface reflects towering cliffs and crags of granite on its eastern shore, and stately pines and firs stand on its western margin.

The Green River heads near Fremont's Peak, in the Wind River Mountains. This river, like the Grand, has its sources in alpine lakes fed by everlasting snows. Thousands of these little lakes, with deep, cold, emerald waters, are embosomed among the crags of the Rocky Mountains. These streams, born in the cold, gloomy solitudes of the upper mountain region, have a strange, eventful history as they pass down through gorges, tumbling in cascades and cataracts, until they reach the hot, arid plains of the Lower Colorado, where the waters that were so clear above empty as turbid floods into the Gulf of California.

The Green River is larger than the Grand and is the upper continuation of the Colorado. Including this river, the whole length of the stream is about 2,000 miles. The region of country drained by the Colorado and its tributaries is about 800 miles in length and varies from 300 to 500 miles in width, containing about 300,000 square miles, an area larger than all the New England and Middle States with Maryland, Virginia and West Virginia added, or nearly as large as Minnesota, Wisconsin, Iowa, Illinois, and Missouri combined.

The upper region, extending to the headwaters of the Grand and Green Rivers, constitutes the great Plateau Province. These plateaus are drained by the Colorado River and its tributaries; the eastern and southern margin by the Rio Grande and its tributaries, and the western by streams that flow into the Great Basin and are lost in the Great Salt Lake and other bodies of water that have no drainage to the sea. The general surface of this upper region is from 5,000 to 8,000 feet above sea level, though the channels of the streams are cut much lower.

This high region, on the east, north, and west, is set with ranges of snow-clad mountains attaining an altitude above the sea varying from 8,000 to 14,000 feet. All winter long snow falls on its mountain-crested rim, filling the gorges, half burying the forests, and covering the crags and peaks with a mantle woven by the winds from the waves of the sea. When the summer sun comes this snow melts and tumbles down the mountain sides in millions of cascades. A million cascade brooks unite to form a thousand torrent creeks; a thousand torrent creeks unite to form half a hundred rivers beset with cataracts; half a hundred roaring rivers unite to form the Colorado, which rolls, a mad, turbid stream, into the Gulf of California.

Consider the action of one of these streams. Its source is in the mountains, where the snows fall; its course, through the arid plains. Now, if at the river's flood storms were falling on the plains, its channel would be cut but little faster than the adjacent country would be washed, and the general level would thus be preserved; but under the conditions here mentioned, the river continually deepens its beds; so all the streams cut deeper and still deeper, until their banks are towering cliffs of solid rock. These deep, narrow gorges are called canyons.

For more than a thousand miles along its course the Colorado has cut for itself such a canyon; but at some few points where lateral streams join it the canyon is broken, and these narrow, transverse valleys divide it into a series of canyons.

The Virgen, Kanab, Paria, Escalante, Fremont, San Rafael, Price, and Uinta on the west, the Grand, White, Yampa, San Juan, and Colorado Chiquito on the east, have also cut for themselves such narrow winding gorges, or deep canyons. Every river entering these has cut another canyon; every lateral creek has cut a canyon; every brook runs in a canyon; every rill born of a shower and born again of a shower and living only during these showers has cut for itself a canyon; so that the whole upper portion of the basin of the Colorado is traversed by a labyrinth of these deep gorges.

Owing to a great variety of geological conditions, these canyons differ much in general aspect. The Rio Virgen, between Long Valley and the Mormon town of Rockville, runs through Parunuweap Canyon, which is often not more than 20 or 30 feet in width and is from 600 to 1,500 feet deep. Away to the north the Yampa empties into the Green by a canyon that I essayed to cross in the fall of 1868, but was baffled from day to day, and the fourth day had nearly passed before I could find my way down to the river. But thirty miles above its mouth this canyon ends, and a narrow valley with a flood plain is found. Still farther up the stream the river comes down through another canyon, and beyond that a narrow valley is found, and its upper course is now through a canyon and now through a valley. All these canyons are alike changeable in their topographic characteristics.

The longest canyon through which the Colorado runs is that between the mouth of the Colorado Chiquito and the Grand Wash, a distance of 217 miles. But this is separated from another above, sixty-five miles in length, only by the narrow canyon valley of the Colorado Chiquito.

All the scenic features of this canyon land are on a giant scale, strange and weird. The streams run at depths almost inaccessible, lashing the rocks which beset their channels, rolling in rapids and plunging in falls, and making a wild music which but adds to the gloom of the solitude. The little valleys nestling along the streams are diversified by bordering willows, clumps of box elder, and small groves of cottonwood.

Low mesas, dry, treeless, stretch back from the brink of the canyon, often showing smooth surfaces of naked, solid rock. In some places the country rock is composed of marls, and here the surface is a bed of loose, disintegrated material through which one walks as in a bed of ashes. Often these marls are richly colored and variegated. In other places the country rock is a loose sandstone, the disintegration of which has left broad stretches of drifting sand, white, golden, and vermilion. Where this sandstone is a conglomerate, a paving of pebbles has been left—a mosaic of many colors, polished by the drifting sands and glistening in the sunlight.

After the canyons, the most remarkable features of the country are the long lines of cliffs. These are bold escarpments scores or hundreds of miles in length—great geographic steps, often hundreds or thousands of feet in altitude, presenting steep faces of rock, often vertical. Having climbed one of these steps, you may descend by a gentle, sometimes imperceptible, slope to the foot of another. They thus present a series of terraces, the steps of which are well-defined escarpments of rock. The lateral extension of such a line of cliffs is usually very irregular; sharp alient [promontories] are projected on the plains below, and deep recesses are cut into the terraces above. Intermittent streams coming down the cliffs have cut many canyons or canyon valleys, by which the traveler may pass from the plain below to the terrace above. By these gigantic stairways he may ascend to high plateaus, covered with forests of pine and fir.

The region is further diversified by short ranges of eruptive mountains. A vast system of fissures—huge cracks in the rocks to the depths below—extends across the country. From these crevices floods of lava have poured, covering mesas and tablelands with sheets of black basalt. The expiring energies of these volcanic agencies have piled up huge cinder cones that stand along the fissures, red, brown, and black, naked of vegetation, and conspicuous landmarks, set as they are in contrast to the bright, variegated rocks of sedimentary origin.

These canyon gorges, obstructing cliffs, and desert wastes have prevented the traveler from penetrating the country, so that until the Colorado River Exploring Expedition was organized it was almost unknown. In the early history of the country Spanish adventurers penetrated the region and told marvelous stories of its wonders. It was also traversed by priests who sought to convert the Indian tribes to Christianity. In later days, since the region has been under the control of the United States, various government expeditions have penetrated the land. Yet enough had been seen in the earlier days to foment rumor, and many wonderful stories were told in the hunter's cabin and the prospector's camp—stories of parties entering the gorge in boats and being carried down with fearful velocity into whirlpools where all were overwhelmed in the abyss of waters, and stories of underground passages for the great river into which boats had passed never to be seen again. It was currently believed that the river was lost under the rocks for several hundred miles. There were other accounts of great falls whose roaring music could be heard on the distant mountain summits; and there were stories current of parties wandering on the brink of the canyon and vainly endeavoring to reach the waters below, and perishing with thirst at last in sight of the river which was roaring its mockery into their dying ears.

The Indians, too, have woven the mysteries of the canyons into the myths of their religion. Long ago there was a great and wise chief who mourned the death of his wife and would not be comforted, until Tavwoats, one of the Indian gods, came to him and told him his wife was in a happier land, and offered to take him there that he might see for himself, if, upon his return, he would cease to mourn.

The great chief promised. Then Tavwoats made a trail through the mountains that intervene between that beautiful land, the balmy region of the great west, and this, the desert home of the poor Numa. This trail was the canyon gorge of the Colorado. Through it he led him; and when they had returned the deity exacted from the chief a promise that he would tell no one of the trail. Then he rolled a river into the gorge, a mad, raging stream, that should engulf any that might attempt to enter thereby.

THE GRAND CANYON

The Grand Canyon is a gorge 217 miles in length, through which flows a great river with many storm-born tributaries. It has a winding way, as rivers are wont to have. Its banks are vast structures of adamant, piled up in forms rarely seen in the mountains.

Down by the river the walls are composed of black gneiss, slates, and schists, all greatly implicated and traversed by dikes of granite. Let this formation be called the black gneiss. It is usually about 800 feet in thickness.

Then over the black gneiss are found 800 feet of quartzites, usually in very thin beds of many colors, but exceedingly hard, and ringing under the hammer like phonolite. These beds are dipping and unconformable with the rocks above; while they make but 800 feet of the wall or less, they have a geological thickness of 12,000 feet. Set up a row of books aslant; it is ten inches from the shelf to the top of the line of books, but there may be 3 feet of the books measured directly through the leaves. So these quartzites are aslant, and though of great geologic thickness, they make but 800 feet of the wall. Your books may have many-colored bindings and differ greatly in their contents; so these quartzites vary greatly from place to place along the wall, and in many places they entirely disappear. Let us call this formation the variegated quartzite.

Above the quartzites there are 500 feet of sandstones. They are of a greenish hue, but are mottled with spots of brown and black by iron stains. They usually stand in a bold cliff, weathered in alcoves. Let this formation be called the cliff sandstone.

Above the cliff sandstone there are 700 feet of bedded sandstones and limestones, which are massive sometimes and sometimes broken into thin strata. These rocks are often weathered in deep alcoves. Let this formation be called the alcove sandstone.

Over the alcove sandstone there are 1,600 feet of limestone, in many places a beautiful marble, as in Marble Canyon. As it appears along the Grand Canyon it is always stained a brilliant red, for immediately over it there are thin seams of iron, and the storms have painted these limestones with pigments from above. Altogether this is the red-wall group. It is chiefly limestone. Let it be called the red wall limestone.

Above the red wall there are 800 feet of gray and bright red sandstone, alternating in beds that look like vast ribbons of landscape. Let it be called the banded sandstone.

And over all, at the top of the wall, is the Aubrey limestone, 1,000 feet in thickness. This Aubrey has much gypsum in it, great beds of alabaster that are pure white in comparison with the great body of limestone below. In the same limestone there are enormous beds of chert, agates, and carnelians. This limestone is especially remarkable for its pinnacles and towers. Let it be called the tower limestone.

Now recapitulate: The black gneiss below, 800 feet in thickness; the variegated quartzite, 800 feet in thickness; the cliff sandstone, 500 feet in thickness; the alcove sandstone, 700 feet in thickness; the red wall limestone, 1,600 feet in thickness; the banded sandstone, 800 feet in thickness; the tower limestone, 1,000 feet in thickness.

Such are the vertical elements of which the Grand Canyon façade is composed. Its horizontal elements must next be considered. The river meanders in great curves, which are themselves broken into curves of smaller magnitude. The streams that head far back in the plateau on either side come down in gorges and break the wall into sections. Each lateral canyon has a secondary system of laterals, and the secondary canyons are broken by tertiary canyons; so the crags are forever branching, like the limbs of an oak.

That which has been described as a wall is such only in its grand effect. In detail it is a series of structures separated by a ramification of canyons, each having its own walls. Thus, in passing down the canyon it seems to be enclosed by walls, but oftener by alient— towering structures that stand between canyons that run back into the plateau. Sometimes gorges of the second or third order have met before reaching the brink of the Grand Canyon, and then great alient are cut off from the wall and stand out as buttes—huge pavilions in the architecture of the canyon. The scenic elements thus described are fused and combined in very different ways.

Stand at some point on the brink of the Grand Canyon where you can overlook the river, and the details of the structure, the vast labyrinth of gorges of which it is composed, are scarcely noticed; the elements are lost in the grand effect, and a broad, deep, flaring gorge of many colors is seen. But stand down among these gorges and the landscape seems to be composed of huge vertical elements of wonderful form. Above, it is an open, sunny gorge; below, it is deep and gloomy. Above, it is a chasm; below, it is a stairway from gloom to heaven.

Thus the elements of the façade of the Grand Canyon change vertically and horizontally. The details of structure can be seen only at close view, but grand effects of structure can be witnessed in great panoramic scenes. Seen in detail, gorges and precipices appear; seen at a distance, in comprehensive views, vast massive structures are presented. The traveler on the brink looks from afar and is over-whelmed with the sublimity of massive forms; the traveler among the gorges stands in the presence of awful mysteries, profound, solemn, and gloomy.

The Grand Canyon of the Colorado is a canyon composed of many canyons. It is a composite of thousands, of tens of thousands, of gorges. In like manner, each wall of the canyon is a composite structure, a wall composed of many walls, but never a repetition. Every one of these almost innumerable gorges is a world of beauty in itself. In the Grand Canyon there are thousands of gorges like that below Niagara Falls, and there are a thousand Yosemites. Yet all these canyons unite to form one grand canyon, the most sublime spectacle on the earth. Pluck up Mt. Washington by the roots to the level of the sea and drop it headfirst into the Grand Canyon, and the dam will not force its waters over the walls. Pluck up the Blue Ridge and hurl it into the Grand Canyon, and it will not fill it.

The wonders of the Grand Canyon cannot be adequately represented in symbols of speech, nor by speech itself. The resources of the graphic art are taxed beyond their powers in attempting to portray its features. Language and illustration combined must fail. The elements that unite to make the Grand Canyon the most sublime spectacle in nature are multifarious and exceedingly diverse. The Cyclopean forms which result from the sculpture of tempests through ages too long for man to compute, are wrought into endless details, to describe which would be a task equal in magnitude to that of describing the stars of the heavens or the multitudinous beauties of the forest with its traceries of foliage presented by oak and pine and poplar, by beech and linden and hawthorn, by tulip and lily and rose, by fern and moss and lichen. Besides the elements of form, there are elements of color, for here the colors of the heavens are rivaled by the colors of the rocks. The rainbow is not more replete with hues. But form and color do not exhaust all the divine qualities of the Grand Canyon. It is the land of music. The river thunders in perpetual roar, swelling in floods of music when the storm gods play upon the rocks and fading away in soft and low murmurs when the infinite blue of heaven is unveiled. With the melody of the great tide rising and falling, swelling and vanishing forever, other melodies are heard in the gorges of the lateral canyons, while the waters plunge in the rapids among the rocks or leap in great cataracts. Thus the Grand Canyon is a land of song. Mountains of music swell in the rivers, hills of music billow in the creeks, and meadows of music murmur in the rills that ripple over the rocks. Altogether it is a symphony of multitudinous melodies. All this is the music of waters. The adamant foundations of the earth have been wrought into a sublime harp, upon which the clouds of the heavens play with mighty tempests or with gentle showers.

The glories and the beauties of form, color, and sound unite in the Grand Canyon—forms unrivaled even by the mountains, colors that vie with sunsets, and sounds that span the diapason from tempest to tinkling raindrop, from cataract to bubbling fountain. But more: it is a vast district of country. Were it a valley plain it would make a state. It can be seen only in parts from hour to hour and from day to day and from week to week and from month to month. A year scarcely suffices to see it all. It has infinite variety, and no part is ever duplicated. Its colors, though many and complex at any instant, change with the ascending and declining sun; lights and shadows appear and vanish with the passing clouds, and the changing seasons mark their passage in changing colors. You cannot see the Grand Canyon in one view, as if it were a changeless spectacle from which a curtain might be lifted, but to see it you have to toil from month to month through its labyrinths. It is a region more difficult to traverse than the Alps or the Himalayas, but if strength and courage are sufficient for the task, by a year's toil a concept of sublimity can be obtained never again to be equaled on the hither side of Paradise.

APPENDIX 2

The Bill Hawkins Account

In the spring of 1884, a young but frail man named William Wallace Bass was told by his physician to move to the Southwest to take advantage of the desert air. Bass built a small cabin on the rim of the Grand Canyon, where the Supai Indians showed him a reliable water supply and an Indian track which he named the Mystic Spring Trail. This rustic camp soon served as a haven for photographers, artists, writers, and geologists from around the world. Bass later built a rock cabin on the river, as well as a crude wooden boat for crossing it.

During its thirty-six-year history, thousands of visitors flocked here, including such famous personalities as writer Zane Grey, artist Thomas Moran, naturalist John Muir, industrialist Henry Ford, and Army Lieutenant Joseph Ives, among many others.

Bass had previously been frustrated by USGS topographic maps which contained Major John Wesley Powell's name as the head of the agency. Bass had also become personally acquainted with Powell, and he wrote of his reasons for distrusting the Major:

"Up to this time I had never met him [Powell] and when in 1887 he employed me as guide in some triangulation work on the Bill Williams Mountain I was thoroughly convinced as to the doubtful character of certain statements he made to me regarding other work of the same nature he claimed to have done some years previous. One in particular was as to a station he said I would find on 'Red Butte,' which lies about forty-five miles northeast of Williams and is a prominent feature on the landscape.... As I had spent considerable time there only a few days previous in looking for a silver prospect reported to be there, I knew there was no such pile of rocks as he described....

"These incidents will explain, in great measure, my suspicions and questions as to anything related by Major Powell. Accordingly, when I secured a copy of the Government publication entitled: 'Exploration of the Colorado River of the West and its Tributaries, Explored in 1869, 1870, 1871 and 1872, under the Direction of the Secretary of the Smithsonian Institution,' and found it was written by Powell, it did not have the same weight with me that it would have done had I not had these personal experiences with him."

When Bass discovered that the Powell monument on the south rim of the Grand Canyon omitted the names of the Howland brothers and Dunn, he was incensed. In 1920 he published a small book, *Adventures in the Canyons of the Colorado: By Two of its Earliest Explorers, James White and W. W. Hawkins*, in an attempt to set the record straight. His inquiry concerned what really happened among the members of the Powell expedition. He interviewed Bill Hawkins about his view of the events that seems to be distorted by Powell and his sympathizers. Bass wrote:

"This [Major Powell's official report of the expedition] is practically the whole story as told by Powell. For years it has been accepted as the truth. Science is Truth focalized, and there is no real science without truth. I have always wondered whether this narrative [by Powell] gave us the whole truth, and when I saw the Powell Monument and noted the omission of the three names of the two Howlands and Dunn, I wondered still more. Why should the names of these three men be left off after having traveled over four hundred miles on the maiden trip, and thus having proven their valor and courage?

"But now comes another witness on the scene. Some time ago I learned that William W. Hawkins, the cook referred to by Powell, was still alive. Powell died in 1902 at the age of 69 years. Hawkins was then living, and thus became the sole survivor (I believe) of the first Powell trip. After the expedition he settled in Pine Valley, Utah, but later moved to Gila Valley, Arizona, and thence to Graham County, where he resided for thirty-five years. He was Justice of the Peace for many years and resided at Eden in that county. He also was a prominent rancher and at his death had six sons living, two of whom reside near Mesa, Arizona. He was highly respected by all who knew him and no one of his large circle of friends and acquaintances will question the truth of this account as given to me for publication. He died in September, 1919, at the St. Joseph's Hospital, Phoenix, Arizona.

"The following account was written by him, in his own handwriting, a few months before his death, at my solicitation, with the understanding that I was to publish it, if it was deemed desirable. Hence I now give it to the world. The following is Hawkins' own brief introduction to his narrative:

'I [Bill Hawkins] will write this as it comes to me and you can then take what portion you may see fit. I will state it just as it happened, at the time it did happen. It seems that you have the two expeditions mixed that Powell made down the Colorado River, and in order to straighten this out it will be necessary for me to give you a brief account of our first expedition from start to finish, then you will have a clear idea of the matter and I can give you a better understanding by commencing at the first.

'Of course this [account] will be [repeating] some that has already been published by Powell himself, and some [events] that happened that was not well to put into Powell's report, but they are true. But as I am the only one that remains of the first expedition I could not prove just how things were and how they happened.

'In the fall of 1868, myself, J. C. Sumner, William Dunn, O. G. Howland and Seneca Howland, brothers, were camped at the Hot Springs in Middle Park, Colorado, about one hundred miles west of Denver, Colorado. We were trapping and prospecting, both in that section and on White River, some seventy-five miles further west. While our party, J. C. Sumner in charge, was in camp at this place, Major Powell and party pulled in with their pack animals, twenty-five animals and twelve or eighteen men. After they stopped and unpacked we all went over to see what they were going to do in this wild country, and they all seemed to be equally interested in our party. Our mode of dress was somewhat different to what they had been used to seeing, as we were all dressed in buckskin, and our hair came down on our shoulders. I was the youngest one in the crowd. We soon found out each other's business.

'Powell told us he intended to make his winter camp over on White River and in the spring he was going to explore the Colorado River from start to finish. We told him that we intended to do the same thing, only on a small scale. He said that only one of his crowd was going with him down the river, that was his brother, Walter Powell. He said he would like to have our party join him and go with him down the river. We had most of our provisions on White River at that time. This was Powell's first trip with his pack animals and it would be necessary for him to make another trip, as most of his party would winter with him.

'After we both got over on White River where our cabins were, he said he would buy our provisions, horses and mules and our traps, and that we could become members of his party and that he would pay us reasonable wages to come with him. So we all agreed on prices for different articles. I had four head of animals, Sumner five head, Dunn two, and the Howland brothers had three head. I owned all the traps. These he was to replace when we got through at Cottonwood Island. So we went to work building more cabins and put up ten or twelve, and fixed up for the winter by dragging up wood, which was plentiful there. Then we laid in a fine supply of venison.

'Before the snow got too deep, Powell took the most of his party that came from the east with him out to Green River Station and he with them went east, leaving his wife and brother in camp. In April we all broke camp and went to Green River Station and made camp about one-half mile below the U. P. R. R. bridge, and waited for Powell to return with our boats, which he did the latter part of April. He sent all the horses to Echo Canyon and sold them. He drew his rations from Fort Bridger.

'We all then went to calking up and painting our boats, which was no small job for us, for we knew nothing about a boat. Powell got a man discharged out of the army at Fort Bridger to come and show us how to calk the boats. This man's name was George Bradley, a man of nerve and staying qualities, as he proved later on.

'Mrs. Powell went to Salt Lake City before going east. We were all anxious to get started, but little did we know what was in store for us in the way of experience and danger. We had four boats, three of them were 22 feet long, 4 feet wide and 3 feet deep. Each end was decked over 4 feet at each end, air tight. These three were supposed to carry the provisions for ten men for eighteen months, that being the time Powell was going to take to make the trip. He was going to winter somewhere in the Canyon. His boat was sixteen feet long, made of pine; the others were oak. They were of the Whitehall pattern. The men were assigned to their boats and then the loads were placed in them.

'The Major's boat was used for a guide boat. It was manned by J. C. Sumner and William Dunn and the Major; next was Walter Powell and Bradley; the next was the Howland brothers and Frank Goodman; the next was the cook boat, manned by myself and Andy Hall. Each boat was loaded so as to have a nearly equal distribution, so that in case of an accident to one of them the others would still have an assortment of the provisions. After each boat had received its load we were ready to start. But where, none of us knew, only that we were going to go down through the Grand Canyon of the Colorado River. We had been told that in places the water ran under the ground.

'There was a great many people on the bank of the river [at Green River Station, Wyoming] to see us start. We were all green at the business, Bradley was the only one that had any experience. But he acknowledged afterwards that this was a little rough. We had very good water for some twenty miles, but, of course, had to watch out for the small boat, as it was supposed to go where the other boats that were loaded could not go. I remember our first camp that evening for the night and as I was steering the boat with one oar behind and standing up I could see what was in front of us. I saw that they were all landing and I told Andy [Hall] they were camping at this point.

'The river was straight and the water smooth and Powell signaled to me and we tried to land, and did finally get to shore some four hundred yards below and the other boats dropped down to where we were and the rest of the boys had the laugh on us. Andy and I told the Major that we were too heavily loaded, the water only lacking four inches from running over the sides of our boat, and as Andy said the next day, we were seven inches nearer the bottom of the river than the other two large boats, as they were nine inches above water, and that we better unload some of the bacon and take chances of replacing it with venison and mountain sheep later on. So we unloaded five hundred pounds of bacon in the river.

'We soon found out that was better. We now passed through Brown's Park, some forty miles from where we started. At the lower end of this park the river now runs into a bad canyon of red sandstone. This was our first canyon and Powell named it the flaming gorge, and it was well named. We made many portages and it was twenty-five miles long. It required ten days to go that distance, as we had to make a trail and carry our provisions and instruments from one place to the other the entire distance, and let the boats down by ropes over the bad rapids. Of course, when we got through and loaded up again the boats were not so heavy and the Major said our appetites were growing.

'At the mouth of this canyon we came to a nice little island which we called Island Park. Here we camped a few days, for we sure had rolled many a rock two-thirds of the twenty-five miles and soaked our provisions. I went out on the east side of the canyon some three miles to see if there was any game and run across a big buck deer coming down the trail to water about one-half mile from camp. He stopped to take a look at me and I shot just as he stopped and broke his neck. The boys heard the shot and Hall and Dunn came out and helped me in with it.

'Powell named the mountain Hawkins Mountain. We moved on down the river, which was very good traveling for a ways and then we heard a great roaring below and saw Powell standing on some rocks on the east side of the river. He motioned us to land, which we all succeeded in doing except Howland's boat. It went over the rapids [Disaster Falls] and broke in two and threw the men out. They succeeded in catching hold of a large pine tree that was drifting top down stream and seemed to stop just to let the boys crawl on to it. The river was raising fast and Sumner, with the small boat, was trying to reach them, but his two first trials failed and the tree began to move on slowly and Goodman shouted, "Goodbye, boys." But then Sumner threw a line he made to where the boys were on the log, which had moved on down a ways, but he got them in the boat and finally got near enough to catch a rope and was hauled into shore some hundred yards below.

'As we had lost considerable of our provisions and one boat, of course the men had to double up in the other boats. Howland No. 1 [Oramel] came in with Hall and myself, Howland No. 2 [Seneca] went in with Capt. Powell and Bradley, Goodwin went in with Sumner, Dunn and the Major. But as we had good water for some time we finally came to the mouth of—[omitted] Creek. Up this creek about 18 miles is the Uinta Agency. We went up to the agency—Powell, Goodman and myself. It was the 4th day of July and we had dinner with the Indian agent. Here we left Goodman. He said he had all he wanted of the river.

'From here to the junction of the Green River with the Grand River the water is very good, a distance of one hundred miles, which took but a few days to make. The canyon is hard rock and the walls on the west side in some places overhang the water three hundred feet. Back under this shelf was drift-wood and willows at that time, a good home for beaver and otter. We stopped for noon and went into camp near the head of a small rapid and tied our boats to small undergrowth, and, being the cook, I had just started a fire in a nice little cove in the brush and rock.

'I had just got my "mess kit" out of the front of the boat when a wind started up and set the leaves and brush all a-blaze. I gathered up the mess kit and made for the boat. But the blaze beat me to it and had burned the small ropes in two that I had the boats tied with, and they were just moving into the current. I jumped, but missed the boat, and down I went, mess kit and all. I held on to the mess kit until I saw I could not raise with it and so I let it go and came to the top of the water to find the boat some thirty feet from me, and Andy was doing his best to hold it up stream until I could catch it.

'I just caught the boat as it was going into the rapid, but it was not a bad rapid, as the waves were about eight feet high. Bradley, held fast to the side of his boat, was not able to get into it, but went through the rapid and a part of the time his head was under the water. At the lower end of this rapid we stopped, as in our rush we had left the Major behind, and in order to get him out of a place he had got into we took four oars and made a bridge across a crevice in the rocks for him to cross over on. Three of the best hats the boys had were lost in the fire and rapids. We were now at the junction of the Green and Grand Rivers. The walls on the west side are 1,800 feet high, where the rivers come together in a V shape.

'Now our trouble begins, and plenty of bad rapids in the river. Dunn was the one who took the altitudes with the barometer and it was here we had the first real trouble in the party, although Powell had named Dunn the "Dirty Devil." But the rest of the boys looked over that.

'At noon, while we were making a portage and letting the boats over a bad place, the ropes happened to catch Bill Dunn under the arms and came near drowning him, but he managed to catch the ropes and come out. While we were eating our dinner Sumner said that Dunn came near being drowned and the Major's brother made the remark that it would have been but little loss, and the Major spoke up and said that Dunn would have to pay thirty dollars for a watch belonging to him that had been soaked with water and ruined, and if he did not he would have to leave the party.

'Andy Hall and I were down at our boat, I having gone down after a cup and Andy had remained at the boat fitting one of his oars. When we returned to where they were eating Sumner asked me what I thought of the Major's proposition, and I asked him what it was, and he then related what had been said. I asked the Major if that was his desire and he said that it was. I made the remark that a part of his wishes could not be granted, as it was impossible to get out of the Canyon on account of the abrupt walls. He then said that it made no difference whether Dunn got out or not. I then said that I was sorry that Dunn had been jerked into the water and got the watch wet, and that I was sorry he felt that way with one of his party, and the Major seemed to be offended at my remarks and said I had no right to pass on the matter. Also that neither Hall nor myself, in the future of the party, would be expected to say anything, as we were too young. Hall made the remark that we had old heads on our shoulders anyway.

'Before this time everything seemed to be getting along fine, as each man had a certain task, or a certain thing to do, and I was doing the cooking, and I generally found plenty to do. Our meal was ready and we all seated ourselves on the rocks to eat our dinner. Up to this time I had always helped the Major all I could and washed his hand (as he only had one) and generally found him a good place to sit at meals, sometimes a few feet from the rest. But before this it never made any difference to me, but now it did, for, as Andy Hall would say, he raised hell with himself in the break he had made with Dunn.

'I could see that there was a different feeling in the whole party at this time and the Major had sat down several feet from the rest of the party. I poured out each man a cup of coffee and one for him also and we all began to eat. He then asked me why I did not bring him his dinner as I had been doing before and I told him he had just said that he was going to make a change in the outfit and I told him that I had made that change to start the ball rolling, and that he would have to come and get his grub like the rest of the boys. His brother then handed his dinner to him.

'After dinner Sumner asked him if he had changed his mind in regard to Dunn and the watch and he said he had not and that Dunn would either pay for the watch or leave the party. Dunn, Hall, Bradley and myself were near the cook boat and about twenty feet from the Major and Sumner. We could not hear what they were talking about, but we had decided that if Dunn left the party we would go with him. Of course, we expected opposition to what we intended to do, so after we had talked the matter over we wanted Bradley to go and tell the Major what we intended to do. But Bradley decided I had better go and tell him myself, as I had made the plan of going with Dunn.

'I went to where Sumner and the Major were talking, and the two Howland boys were with them. I told the Major that Bradley, Hall and myself had decided to go with Dunn and that we would take my boat (the cook boat) and some grub, and we would pull out, and he could come when he got ready. He said he would not stand any such work, that it would be the ruin of his party. I told him that it was all his own fault and that I had no more talk to make and went back to the boat.

'I found Dunn, Bradley and Hall waiting to see what had happened, but before I had time to tell them, Sumner came and began to talk to us, telling us to not feel put out, that the Major was hasty and to give him another chance. Dunn said that the Major never did like him anyway, if he had he would never have named the Eskalanty [Escalante] River dirty devil. We camped at that place for the night and in the morning the Major said he would take thirty dollars for the watch and that he could pay for it when we got through. None of the party except the Major liked Capt. Powell. He had a bulldozing way that was not then practiced in the west. He threatened to slap me several times for trying to sing like he did, but he never did slap anyone in the party.

'We all moved off down the river all O.K., but our provisions began to run short, rapids became more often, some of them very bad, but for a few days everything went all right. The boys would tell Indian adventures at night that someone had had, but the remark was made that Dunn had nothing to say and Captain Powell said he guessed Dunn did not know much about Indians. The Major chipped in and said, nor anything else. Sumner took it up for Dunn because he knew there would soon be trouble, and told Powell that Dunn had been wounded four times by the Comanches, so it all passed off.

'The next day we had some very bad rapids, so bad that it was necessary to let the boats around some large rocks, and in order to do this, and as Dunn was a fine swimmer, the Major asked him to swim out to a rock where he could catch the rope and raise it over the rock so the boat would swing in below. He made the rock all O.K. and was ready to catch the rope which was supposed to be thrown to him, so he could swing the boat in below, but the Major saw his chance to drown Dunn, as we thought, and he held to the rope. That was the first time that he had interfered in the letting the boats around bad places and the rope caught Dunn around the legs and pulled him into the current and came near losing the boat. But Dunn held on to the rope and finally stopped in water up to his hips. We were all in the water but the Major and Captain Dunn told the Major that if he had not been a good swimmer he and the boat both would have been lost.

'The Major said as to Dunn that there would have been but little loss. One word brought on another, and the Major called Dunn a bad name and Dunn said that if the Major was not a cripple he would not be called such names. Then Captain Powell said he was not crippled and started for Dunn with an oath, and the remark he would finish Dunn. He had to pass right by me and I knew that he would soon drown Dunn, as he, so much larger, could easily do. He was swearing and his eyes looked like fire and just as he passed I caught him by the hair of his head and pulled him over back into the water.

'Howland saw us scuffling and he was afraid Cap would get hold of my legs, but Dunn got to me first and said, For God's sake,

Bill, you will drown him. By that time Howland was there and Cap had been in the water long enough and Dunn and Howland drug him out on the sand bar in the rocks. After I got my hold in Cap's hair I was afraid to let go, for he was a very strong man. He was up in a short time, and mad! I guess he was mad! He cursed me to everything, even to being a "Missouri Puke." I wasn't afraid of him when I got on dry ground; I could out-knock him after he was picked up twice.

'He made for his gun and swore he would kill me and Dunn. But this talk did not excite me and as he was taking his gun from the deck of the boat Andy Hall gave him a punch behind the ear and told him to put it back or off would go his head. Cap looked around and saw who had the gun and he sure dropped his. This all happened before the Major got around to where we were. He soon took in the situation and came to me and made the remark that he would have never thought that I would go back on him. I told him that he had gone back on himself and that he had better help Cap get the sand out of his eyes, that if he monkeyed with me any more I would keep him down next time.

'Sumner and I had all we could do to keep down mutiny and there was bad feeling from that time on for a few days and we began to not recognize any authority from the Major. We began to run races with our boats, as the loads were almost all gone. It was fun for the first two days, but the water began to get rough. Hall, Howland and myself were in my boat and I had become an expert in bad rapids and we ran several that the other two boats were let over with ropes. We stopped at noon one day to wait for the other boats. We were at the head of four bad rapids; it was some two hours before the other boats came and I had coffee all ready, as that was our principal food then.

'We had but little flour, but had plenty of dried apples and coffee. We laid in camp that afternoon and the Major and Sumner spent that afternoon in trying to find a place where we could let the boats over the first rapid with ropes. But they failed to find any place where we could get footing enough and the walls were too high for our ropes, so the Major said we would try to find a place on the west side the next day. That evening late Major and Sumner and the two Howland boys held a consultation (as I afterwards found out) to see about leaving the river with all hands.

'He said we would cross over and leave our boats and instruments under some large rocks and that we then would go out to some Mormon settlements and get some grub and return to our boats and continue on down the river. The Major asked me to bake up all the flour that we had and said to make the bread into biscuits, or dough-gods (as we called them), as flour and water was what we had to make them with. In about three hours I had them all baked. I told the Major that the bread was ready and he called the boys and told them all his intentions as to leaving the river. That was the first time Hall and I knew anything about what was going on. I told Hall to take our shares and put them in the boat, as the Major said that each man should keep his own part as we might get separated.

'I told the Major that Hall and I had no intention of separating, and that Bradley, Hall and myself were going to stay with the river and go through or drown. I also told him that if we had enough coming to us to pay for the boat that he could keep it. Dunn, O. G. Howland and Seneca Howland had made up their minds to go and Dunn said he hated to leave Hall and myself, as we had been together a long time, and that we would perish in the river and that we had better come and stay with the party.

'I told him that was what I was doing, that I called Hall, Bradley and myself a party of three and each one of them was a party of one. While we were talking the Major came up to me and laid his left arm across my neck, tears running down his cheeks. By that time the rest of the boys were present and the Major said to me, Bill, do you really mean what you say?

'I told him that I did, and he said that if he had one man that would stay with him that he would not abandon the river, I just simply said that he did not know his party, and that Andy Hall and myself were too young to have any say in council and I said we are off now. He said that it was near noon and if I would make some coffee that we would have a cup of coffee together. I have been present at many solemn occasions, but I never witnessed one that come up to this.

'There were some strong hearts that shed tears. Bradley said it made him a child again. We crossed over to the west side of the river and there was where we left our instruments and one boat. This is the last time we ever saw Dunn and the two Howland brothers alive.

'Some years afterwards I, with a party of some others, buried their bones in the Shewits [Shivwits] Mountains, below Kanab wash. As to Powell leaving the party at Lees Ferry, there was no ferry on the river, no one except some Indians ever crossed. There was no place known as Kanab wash when we first came down. Powell never left the party until we got through to the mouth of the Virgin River, where he and his brother were taken to the railroad or stage by some Mormons who lived on the Muddy. Sumner, Bradley, Hall and myself continued on down the river. Hall and I stopped at Ehrenburg and Sumner and Bradley went on to Yuma. From there Sumner went to Denver and Bradley to San Diego, where he died.

'Sumner died at Vernal, Utah, so I heard, and Hall was killed near Globe, Arizona. Powell and his brother both died somewhere in the east and I am here nine miles below Phoenix.

[Signed] W. W. HAWKINS'"

[*Note*: Additional paragraphing has been added and minor misspelling corrected in an attempt to improve readability.]

APPENDIX 3

The James White Story

THE CASE FOR JAMES WHITE

The vast majority of those who have examined the bold claim of James White to be the first individual to navigate the Colorado River through the Grand Canyon are, to put it bluntly, unpersuaded. This includes such notable critics as Major Powell and his chief boatman Jack Sumner, as well as noted historian and *Colorado River Controversies* author Robert Brewster Stanton, who believed that White was simply confused and only traveled from the Grand Wash Cliffs at the end of the Grand Canyon to Callville, Nevada.

But a longtime resident of the Grand Canyon named William Wallace Bass was convinced that White completed the journey, and he wrote the following defense of White in his small book, *Adventures in the Canyons of the Colorado: By Two of its Earliest Explorers, James White and W. W. Hawkins*, published in 1920:

"It seems to be a natural trait for any man, no matter how great, to claim to have been first in any great endeavor, dangerous exploration or unusual undertaking. Hence it was to be expected that after Major Powell had made his memorable first trip down the Canyons of the Colorado that he and his friends should assert that his was the first expedition to attempt this hazardous undertaking.

"Yet, while it may appear strange, an account appeared in the Rocky Mountain Herald of the date of January 8, 1869, about five months before Major Powell started on his first expedition, giving circumstantial detail of the passage on a raft through the Canyons of the Colorado from the San Juan River, by a Wisconsin prospector, James White.

"More dead than alive, he emerged from the lower reaches of the Canyon at Callville, a Mormon settlement, where he was cared for and nursed back to life. Mr. White is still alive, a respected and honored old man, a citizen of Trinidad, Colorado, and while all the writers that have extolled Powell, from George Wharton James down to the Kolb Bros., have either abused or ignored White, there is a growing conviction that the old man's story was and is true and that he did actually make the journey.

"A stalwart defender of White appeared in 1917 in the person of Mr. Thomas F. Dawson, who succeeded in having the Senate of the U.S. Congress publish an elaborate argument of some sixty-seven pages which he had prepared, entitled: 'The Grand Canyon—An article giving the credit of first traversing the Grand Canyon of the Colorado to James White, a Colorado gold prospector, who it is claimed made the voyage two years previous to the expedition under the direction of Maj. J. W. Powell in 1869.

"This pamphlet called forth a strong rejoinder from Robert Brewster Stanton, which occupied some twenty-two pages of The Trail, a monthly publication of the Sons of Colorado. In it, this eminent engineer and writer, whose intimate knowledge of the Canyon none can dispute, while giving full credit to the honesty and integrity of Mr. White, still insists that he was unintentionally wrong in the main part of his statements. On the other hand, F. S. Dellenbaugh, who has written two books on the Colorado River, viz., The Romance of the Colorado River and A Canyon Voyage, openly assails White as a mendacious fabricator of the worst type.

"It would not be impossible for me, with my intimate personal knowledge of one portion of the Grand Canyon, extending over a period of nearly forty years, to point out discrepancies and inaccuracies in the published statements of both Stanton and Dellenbaugh, but it is not worth while here to do this. Personally, I have come to believe White's statements, and here wish to reproduce in facsimile a letter he wrote to his brother, dated Callville, September 26, 1867. Owing to the imperfections in spelling, punctuation, etc., I give a rendition (made by Mr. Dawson) into correct English.

NAVIGATION OF THE BIG CANYON—
A TERRIBLE VOYAGE

Callville, September 26, 1867.

Dear brother:

It has been some time since I have heard from you. I got no answer from the last letter I wrote you, for I left soon after I wrote. I went prospecting with Captain Baker and George Stroll in the San Juan mountains. We found very good prospects, but nothing that would pay.

Then we started down the San Juan River. We traveled down about 200 miles; then we crossed over on the Colorado and camped. We laid over one day. We found that we could not travel down the river, and our horses had sore feet. We had made up our minds to turn back when we were attacked by fifteen or twenty Ute Indians. They killed Baker, and George Stroll and myself took four ropes off our horses, an axe, ten pounds of flour and our guns.

We had fifteen miles to walk to the Colorado. We got to the river just at night. We built a raft that night. We sailed all that night. We had good sailing for three days; the fourth day George Stroll was washed off the raft and drowned, and that left me alone. I thought that it would be my time next. I then pulled off my pants and boots. I then tied a rope to my waist. I went over falls from ten to fifteen feet high. My raft would tip over three or four times a day.

The third day we lost our flour, and for seven days I had nothing to eat except a raw-hide knife cover. The eighth day I got some mesquite beans. The thirteenth day I met a party of friendly Indians. They would not give me anything to eat, so I gave them my pistol for the hind parts of a dog. I had one of them for supper and the other for breakfast.

The sixteenth day I arrived at Callville, where I was taken care of by James Ferry. I was ten days without pants or boots or hat. I was sun-burnt so I could hardly walk. The Indians took seven head of horses from us. I wish I could write you half I underwent. I saw the hardest time that any man ever did in the world, but thank God that I got through it safe.

I am well again, and I hope these few lines will find you all well. I send my best respects to all. Josh, answer this when you get it. Direct your letter to Callville, Arizona. Ask Tom to answer that letter I wrote him several years ago.

[Signed] JAMES WHITE.

"Stanton claims that White only went through the lower part of the Canyon, viz., from the Grand Wash Cliffs to Callville. This much he concedes, and he asserts that the evidence is clear that White was led to claim he had traveled the whole length of the Canyons, not through dishonesty, but by the law of suggestion.

"The men with whom he talked, after he was rescued from the raft, knowing little or nothing of the Canyon, and assuming he had traveled the whole distance from the San Juan, made him believe he had so traveled. When his terrible physical and mental condition is recalled, it is not hard to believe that he was in such a weakened state as readily to receive any powerful mental suggestion, and that this, once firmly fixed in his mind, ever afterwards appeared to him to be the strict and literal truth.

"But this assertion of Stanton's implies that White and his companion, Stroll, after Captain Baker was killed, crossed the intervening hundreds of miles from the San Juan to the head of the Grand Wash, and that he there entered the Canyon and floated down to Callville. To my limited intelligence it seems incredible that any man could believe in the truth and honesty of James White and yet not question him as to how he forgot to mention how he traveled over all these hundreds of miles.

"White never makes a word of reference to it, nor does Stanton. Did White come on a flying machine in a trance? Let anyone, even though he be unfamiliar with the wild country that exists between the San Juan and the Grand Wash, look at a U.S. Geological Survey map and he will then be able to form some idea of the practical difficulties in the way of anyone crossing it. Then, when it is recalled, that White was beset by hostile Indians, who were determined to slay him and capture his outfit; that the country was unknown to him; that there was no food except that which he could secure with his rifle, is it not evident that he would far rather take his chances on facing the unknown dangers of the river than face certain death at the hands of the surrounding Indians?

"Personally, it is far harder for me to believe that White came overland, and forgot all about that trip, and entered the Canyon at its lower end, than it is to accept his own plain statement that he built the raft near the junction of the Grand and the Green and made the whole descent of the Colorado River to the point where he was rescued at Callville.

"My first interest in White's trip through the Grand Canyon dates back to 1883, while I was engaged in train service for the Atlantic and Pacific Railroad (now the Santa Fe) during its construction between Williams, Arizona, and the Colorado River where the bridge is now situated near Needles, California. It so happened that we were detained for several days at Kingman, Arizona, due to a fire that destroyed boarding cars and a water tank on the line near the end of the construction work. At this time I had never taken any interest in the Grand Canyon, in fact knew nothing about it, only from vague reports that were being circulated by the railroad men who had been out to see it from Peach Springs, at the mouth of Diamond Creek Canyon.

"This route was then in its infancy and later was opened to visitors and was the first one opened to the public. They were so enthusiastic in their descriptions of this now famous 'National Park' that I at once became very greatly interested, and when I chanced to meet a man named Hardy, who was then in Kingman, I found that he lived on the Colorado River and was engaged in goat raising. He told me about finding some mountain sheep among his band of goats, and various other experiences he had met, not the least of which was finding a man on a raft who had come through the entire Grand Canyon. He described him as being in an exhausted condition and covered with sores festered by flies. After reviving the man they learned the story of his sufferings and the drowning of his partner while going through some bad rapids; in fact his descriptions to me of what White told him was very much the same as has been published from later interviews to different parties."

"This was in July, 1883, when I met Mr. Hardy, and in September following I set out to make my first visit to Grand Canyon, from Williams, Arizona.

"Since that time I have taken a great interest in its history and discovery. F. S. Dellenbaugh, a member of the Powell party of 1872, while on a visit to my camp at Bass Trail, told me his opinion of White's dramatic tale and I later read the same in his *Romance of the Colorado River*, wherein he stamps the whole story as a 'splendid yarn' (and I may here add, 'but well told'). He denounces White's account as an utterly improbable feat to accomplish, but from my first personal knowledge of what the river is at the season of year that White's trip was staged, I cannot agree with Dellenbaugh, and never have. From my many years of observation in this section of the Canyon I am thoroughly convinced that during the period of high water, which is from the last of June until late in August, a raft may pass safely through the entire 488 miles of the canyon without disaster. It would be dangerous in the extreme in low water.

"Another incident to strengthen my belief in White's story was the meeting of a man, J. P. Vollmer by name, then president of the First National Bank of Lewiston, Idaho, who was a visitor to the canyon some years later. He told me he came near being a member of White's party when they were about to start on their prospecting trip on the Mancos in Colorado, but unavoidably he was prevented from joining them in time or he might have been among them when attacked by the Utes and met the fate of Baker, or with White and his partner on the raft.

"I subsequently corresponded with Vollmer regarding the incident and he once wrote me he was quite sure he could find some record of dates among his papers, but later on failed to do so. He and various others with whom I have talked regarding White have all united in their convictions of the truth of White's claims regarding this, the first journey through the entire five divisions of canyons through which the Colorado River maintains its tortuous existence, 218 miles of which, at the western end, is known as the Grand Canyon."

[Signed] W. W. BASS.
Grand Canyon, Arizona, May 21st, 1920."

[*Note*: Additional paragraphing has been added and minor misspelling corrected in order to improve readability.]

THE CASE AGAINST JAMES WHITE

Chief among the critics of James White and his claim to be the first to traverse the Colorado River through the Grand Canyon was Frederick S. Dellenbaugh, a member of Powell's second expedition and one of the Major's greatest admirers. In his book, *A Canyon Voyage* (1908), Dellenbaugh explains why White's journey was simply impossible:

"The following year, 1867, a man [James White] was picked up at Callville, in an exhausted and famishing condition, by a frontiersman named Hardy. When he had been revived he told his story. It was that he had come on a raft through the Grand Canyon above, and all the canyons antecedent to that back to a point on Grand River. The story was apparently straightforward, and it was fully accepted. At last, it was thought, a human being has passed through this Valley of the Shadow of Death and lived to tell of its terrors.

"Hardy took him down to Fort Mohave, where he met Dr. Parry, who recorded his whole story, drawn out by many questions, and believed it. This was not surprising; for, no man ever yet having accomplished what White claimed to have done, there was no way of checking the points of his tale. 'Now, at last,' remarks Dr. Parry, 'we have a perfectly authentic account, from an intelligent source, from a man who actually traversed its formidable depths, and who,

fortunately for science, still lives to detail his trustworthy observations of this remarkable voyage.' The doctor was too confiding.

"Had I the space I would give here the whole of White's story,
for it is one of the best bits of fiction I have ever read. He had
obtained somehow a general smattering of the character of the river,
but as there were trappers still living, Kit Carson, for example, who
possessed a great deal of information about it, this was not a difficult matter. But that he had no exact knowledge of any part of the
river above the lower end of the Grand Canyon, is apparent to one
who is familiar with the ground, and the many discrepancies brand
the whole story as a fabrication. In the language of the frontier, he
'pitched a yarn,' and it took beautifully. Hardy, whom I met in Arizona a good many years ago, told me he believed the man told the
truth, but his belief was apparently based only on the condition
White was in when rescued. That he was nearly dead is true, but
that is about all of his yarn that is.

"White was thirty-two years old, and from Kenosha, Wisconsin. He said that, with two others, he was prospecting in Southwestern Colorado in the summer of that year, 1867, when, on Grand
River, they were attacked by the Utes. Baker, the leader, fell mor-
tally wounded. Of course, White and the other man, Strole, stood
by their leader, in the teeth of the enemy's fire, till he expired. What
would the story have been without this example of devotion and fortitude? Then, holding the pursuers in check, they slowly retreated
down the side canyon they were in to the main gorge, where they
discovered an abundance of driftwood, and decided to make a raft
with which to escape. This raft consisted of three sticks of cottonwood about ten feet long and eight inches diameter, tied together
with lariats.

"They had abandoned their horses above, bringing only their
arms, ammunition, and some food. Waiting for midnight to come
so that their pursuers might not discover their intention, they seized
their poles and, under the waning moon, cast off, and were soon
on the tempestuous tide, rushing through the yawning chasm.

'Through the long night they clung to the raft as it dashed against half-concealed rocks, or whirled about like a plaything in some eddy.' When daylight came they landed; as they had a smoother current and less rugged banks, though the canyon walls appeared to have increased in height. They strengthened their raft and went on. In the afternoon, after having floated about thirty miles from the starting point they reached the junction of the Grand and Green.

"So far all is well, but here he makes his first break, as he had no conception of the actual character of the rivers at the junction. He says the canyon now far surpassed that of either of the forming streams, which is not so. For five or six miles below the junction there is little change, yet he describes the walls as being four thousand feet high, an altitude never attained in Cataract Canyon at all, the highest being somewhat under three thousand, while at the junction they are only thirteen hundred.

"Then he goes on to say that detached pinnacles appeared to rise 'one above the other,' for one thousand feet more, giving an altitude here of five thousand feet, clearly an impression in his mind of the lower end of the Grand Canyon, which he had doubtless become somewhat familiar with in some prospecting trip. He fancied the 'Great Canyon' began at the junction of the Grand and Green, and he did not appreciate the distance that intervened between Callville and that point. They tied up at night and traveled in the day.

"No mention is made of the terrific rapids which roar in Cataract Canyon, but he speaks of the 'grey sandstone walls' the lower portion smooth from the action of floods. There exist some greyish walls; but most are red except in the granite gorges of the Grand Canyon, where, for a thousand feet, they are black. Below the junction, forty miles, they came to the mouth of the San Juan! Yet Cataract Canyon and Narrow together, the first canyons of the Colorado proper, are fifty miles long and the San Juan comes in at least seventy-five miles below their end. The walls of the San Juan he describes as being as high as those of the Colorado, which he has just been talking about, that is, five thousand feet, yet for these seventy-five miles he would have actually been passing between walls of about one thousand feet. He says he could not escape here because the waters of the San Juan were so violent they filled its canyon from bank to bank. In reality, he could have made his way out of the canyon (Glen Canyon) in a great many places in the long distance between the foot of Narrow Canyon and the San Juan.

"There is nothing difficult about it. But not knowing this, and nobody else knowing it at that time, the yarn went very well. Also, below the San Juan, as far as Lees Ferry, there are numerous opportunities to leave the canyon; and there are a great many attractive bottoms all the way through sunny Glen Canyon, where landings could have been made in a bona fide journey, and birds snared; anything rather than to go drifting along day after day toward dangers unknown. 'At every bend of the river it seemed as if they were descending deeper into the earth, and that the walls were coming closer together above them, shutting out the narrow belt of sky, thickening the black shadows, and redoubling the echoes that went up from the foaming waters,' all of which is nonsense.

"They were not yet, even taking their own, or rather his own, calculations, near the Grand Canyon, and the whole one hundred and forty-nine miles of Glen Canyon are simply charming; altogether delightful. One can paddle along in any sort of craft, can leave the river in many places, and in general enjoy himself. I have been over the stretch twice, once at low water and again at high, so I speak from abundant experience. Naively he remarks, 'as yet they had seen no natural bridge spanning the chasm above them, nor had fall or cataract prevented their safe advance!' Yet they are supposed to have passed through the forty-one miles of Cataract Canyon's turmoil, which I venture to say no man could ever forget. They had been only four days getting to a point below the San Juan, simply drifting; that is about two hundred miles, or some fifty miles a daylight day. Around three o'clock on the fourth day they heard the deep roar as of a waterfall in front of them.

"They felt the raft agitated, then whirled along with frightful rapidity towards a wall that seemed to bar all further progress. As they approached the cliff the river made a sharp bend, around which the raft swept, disclosing to them, in a long vista, the water lashed into foam, as it poured through a narrow precipitous gorge, caused by huge masses of rock detached from the main walls. There was no time to think. The logs strained as if they would break their fastenings. The waves dashed around the men, and the raft was buried in the seething waters.

"White clung to the logs with the grip of death. His comrade stood up for an instant with the pole in his hands, as if to guide the raft from the rocks against which it was plunging; but he had scarcely straightened before the raft seemed to leap down a chasm and, amid the deafening roar of waters, White heard a shriek that thrilled him to the heart, and, looking around, saw, through the mist and spray, the form of his comrade tossed for an instant on the water, then sinking out of sight in a whirlpool.

"On the fifth day White lashed himself to the raft. He then describes a succession of rapids, passing which with great difficulty he reached a stream that he afterward learned was the Little Colorado. He said the canyon was like that of the San Juan, but they are totally different. The current of this stream swept across that of the Colorado, 'causing in a black chasm on the opposite bank a large and dangerous whirlpool.'

"He could not avoid this and was swept by the cross current into this awful place, which, to relieve the reader's anxiety, I hasten to add, does not exist. There is no whirlpool whatever at the mouth of the Little Colorado, nor any other danger. But White now felt that further exertion was useless, and amidst the 'gurgling' waters closed his eyes for some minutes, when, feeling a strange swinging sensation, he opened them and found that he was circling round the whirlpool, sometimes close to the terrible vortex, etc. He thought he fainted. He was nothing if not dramatic. When he recovered it was night.

"Then for the first time he thought of prayer. 'I spoke as if from my very soul, and said: "Oh, God, if there is a way out of this fearful place, show it to me, take me to it."' His narrator says White's voice here became husky and his features quivered. 'I was still looking up with my hands clasped when I felt a different movement of the raft and turning to look at the whirlpool it was some distance behind (he could see it in the night!), and I was floating on the smoothest current I had yet seen in the canyon.'

"The current was now very slow and he found that the rapids were past. The terrible mythical whirlpool at the innocent mouth of the Little Colorado was the end of the turmoil, though he said the canyon went on, the course of the river being exceedingly crooked, and shut in by precipices of white sand rock! There is no white 'sand-rock' in the Grand Canyon.

"All through this terrific gorge wherein the river falls some eighteen hundred feet, White found a slow current and his troubles from rapids were over! For 217 miles of the worst piece of river in the world, he found no difficulty. The gloom and lack of food alone oppressed him, and he thought of plunging from the raft, but lacked the courage. Had he really entered the Grand Canyon his raft would have been speedily reduced to toothpicks and he would not have had the choice of remaining upon it. Finally, he reached a bank upon which some mesquite bushes grew, and he devoured the green pods. Then sailing on in a sort of stupor he was roused by voices and saw some Yampais, who gave him meat and roasted mesquite beans. Proceeding, he heard voices again and a dash of oars. It was Hardy and at last White was saved!

"We have seen various actors passing before us in this drama, but I doubt if any of them have been more picturesque than this champion prevaricator. But he had related a splendid yarn. What it was intended to obscure would probably be quite as interesting as what he told. Just where he entered upon the river is of course impossible to decide, but that he never came through the Grand Canyon is as certain as anything can be. His story reveals an absolute ignorance of the river and its walls throughout the whole course he pretended to have traversed."

[*Note*: Additional paragraphing has been added in an attempt to improve readability.]

SELECTED BIBLIOGRAPHY

Bass, William Wallace. *Adventures in the Canyons of the Colorado.* Grand Canyon, Arizona, 1920.

Darrah, William Culp. *Powell of the Colorado.* Princeton: Princeton University Press, 1951.

Darrah, William Culp, Ralph V. Chamberlain, and Charles Kelly, eds. *The Exploration of the Colorado River in 1869 and 1871–1872.* Salt Lake City: University of Utah Press, 2009.

Dellenbaugh, Frederick A. *A Canyon Voyage: The Narrative of the Second Powell Expedition down the Green-Colorado River from Wyoming, and the Explorations on Land, in the Years 1871 and 1872.* Tucson: University of Arizona Press, 1996.

——. *The Romance of the Colorado River.* Chicago: Rio Grande Press, 1902.

Dolnick, Edward. *Down the Great Unknown: John Wesley Powell's 1869 Journey of Discovery and Tragedy Through the Grand Canyon.* New York: HarperCollins, 2001.

Goldwater, Barry M. *Delightful Journey Down the Green and Colorado Rivers.* Tempe, Arizona: Arizona Historical Foundation, 1970.

Hillers, John. *Photographed All the Best Scenery.* Salt Lake City: University of Utah Press, 1972.

Kolb, Ellsworth L. *Through the Canyon from Wyoming to Mexico.* New York: Macmillan, 1914.

Powell, John Wesley. *The Exploration of the Colorado River and Its Canyons.* New York: Penguin, 1987.

Stanton, Robert B. *Down the Colorado.* Norman: University of Oklahoma Press, 1965.

————. *Colorado River Controversies.* New York: Dodd, Mead, 1932.

Staveley, Gaylord. *Broken Waters Sing: Rediscovering Two Great Rivers of the West.* Boston: Little, Brown, 1971.

Stegner, Wallace. *Beyond the Hundredth Meridian.* New York: Houghton Mifflin, 1954.

Worster, Donald. *A River Running West: The Life of John Wesley Powell.* New York: Oxford University Press, 2001.

INDEX